M000020843

Saving Our Sons

A Parent's Guide to Preparing Boys for Success

CLAYTON LESSOR
MA, LPC

With Lisa Canfield

Saving Our Sons
A Parent's Guide to Preparing Boys for Success
By Clayton Lessor
Quest Project Press

Published by: Quest Project Press, St. Louis, MO

Copyeditor: Nina Durfee, www.ninadurfee.com

Index: Elena Gwynne, www.quillandinkindexing.com

Cover and Interior Design: Davis Creative, www. daviscreative.com

ISBN: 978-0-9963607-0-8

Library of Congress Number: 2015959631

ATTENTION CORPORATIONS, UNIVERSITIES, COLLEGES AND PROFESSIONAL ORGANIZATIONS: Quantity discounts are available on bulk purchases of this book for educational, gift purposes, or as premiums for increasing magazine subscriptions or renewals. Special books or book excerpts can also be created to fit specific needs. For information, please contact Quest Project Press, 8820 Pardee Road, St. Louis, MO 63123.

Dedication

To little Clayton Lessor.
It was never your fault, and
you survived to help so many in need.
Use your gift wisely, as you truly deserve
all good things that life has to offer.

To all of you brave individuals
who have helped, are helping, and will endeavor
to help boys become healthy men.
I offer you this challenge:
make time every day to bless a younger person
with a kind word or acknowledgement.

Table of Contents

I'm Very Glad You Picked up This Book...   1

Chapter 1: Who Is Your Fantasy Son?   5

Chapter 2: The State of Boyhood   9

Chapter 3: What's Missing   27

Chapter 4: When to Contact the Authorities   39

Chapter 5: The Quest Project®   45

Chapter 6: The Quest Project®—An Overview   55

Chapter 7: Case Studies   71

Chapter 8: Dylan   73

Chapter 9: Andrew   85

Chapter 10: Jordan   97

Chapter 11: Ethan   109

Chapter 12: David   121

Chapter 13: Steven   133

Chapter 14: Sam   145

Chapter 15: Joey   159

Chapter 16: Moving Forward   173

Chapter 17: A Little about Me   177

Index   181

Acknowledgements

I appreciate and acknowledge all of you who have participated in my experiences, journey, and growth, especially:

Doris (Mom) and Russell (Dad). Without you I would not have had the childhood experience or the wound that I survived and recovered from. My experience is the gift that drives me to help so many lost and hurt souls.

My grandparents, Ralph and Burnette Boyer, for providing my basic needs every year until I was sixteen. Special thanks to Grandma for bestowing on me your kind spirit.

Clayton Robert Lessor. I carry your name, I know you loved me, and you passed before your time.

Violet Lessor for giving me room and board after my house burned down, pushing me through my depression, and handing me off to the Air Force.

The United States Air Force for nurturing me like a parent and for providing escape from the chaos, discovering my potential, and setting the stage for me to be a successful Man.

My many friends who have come and gone for offering me experiences and character examples to integrate into my being. Jay Loechel, my high school best friend and military enlistment buddy, always looking out for me. Sergeant John Maddux for having my back while I was out of country. Chief Master Sergeant Harry House, Colonel Don Boatright, Tom Muenks (my "older brother from a different mother"), the Honorable Gordon Schweitzer, and my late father-in-law, Don Brown.

Those who have mentored me: Chief Master Sergeant Ray Ford, my first significant healthy mentor and elder who made it clear I had potential to do more; Chris Frey, my first male therapist who nudged me and mentored me through my shit, always giving homework to move me through the pain; Dr. Sam Marwit and Dr. Leone Snyder, my academic mentors and education gurus; and Kathy Poelker a sounding board for my creative ideas.

Lisa Canfield, ghostwriter extraordinaire, for detailing each conversation and developing a succinct conceptual idea with each interview.

Pinot Noir, our six-year-old long-haired mini-dachshund, who has learned to say a prayer every night before bed.

My wife, Debbie, the most important person and love of my life. You stand by me through good times and hard times. You give all that you are for our family. You remind me to keep it straight when I don't want to, and you make me want to be a better man.

I'm Very Glad You Picked up This Book...

...because, if you're the mother of a teenage boy who is going through a rough patch, I know that you need help.

You might need help reaching a person you feel like you don't even know anymore.

You might need help stopping behavior that is putting your child's future in danger.

You might need help understanding why, no matter what you try (and you've tried just about everything), nothing is working.

You might need help figuring out how you can help your son overcome his challenges and become the kind of young man you dream—and know—he can be.

That's why I wrote this book.

As a licensed psychotherapist, I work with all kinds of people and all kinds of issues; facilitating women's and men's groups, counseling couples struggling with marital problems, and working one-on-one with individuals to help them deal with things like anger, depression, or anxiety.

For the past twenty years, however, my real specialty has been working with boys. Especially adolescent boys.

Boys like yours.

Because of this, if you are the mother of a teenage boy, I probably know a few things about you—presumptuous as that might sound. For example, I know you love your son (even if you might not always feel like you do). I know that you want the best for him. I know you work as hard as you can to do the right thing to give your boy what he needs to grow up strong and healthy and happy and whole.

And I also know that, if you're anything like the mothers I meet in my practice, you are discovering that doing any or all of that can be hard.

It's hard for a reason. He's a teenager. I don't think I know any parents who expected the teenage years to be easy. But that's part of the problem. When boys who seem well-adjusted suddenly start behaving differently, it can be hard to spot the difference between normal, irritating, teenage behavior and a genuine problem that needs to be addressed.

So a lot of parents wait, thinking the problem will go away.

And by the time they begin to suspect that their son needs professional help, things have usually gotten worse.

That's the point when mothers typically come into my office. A boy who has always loved school comes home with a failing report card. Or a kindhearted, calm kid becomes belligerent or aggressive—maybe even to the point where he scares his mom. Or a popular, happy boy becomes sullen and withdrawn and spends all his time locked in his room.

You're right to be worried about behaviors like these. Because what most parents don't know is that for every problem they recognize, there may be other, more serious issues hidden below the surface. For example, you might not know if your son is drinking or using drugs. Even if you do know, you probably don't know how much, or how often, or if he's engaging in other types of self-destructive behavior. And what about criminal behavior, like vandalism or shoplifting? You might not know about that until he actually gets caught.

The problem isn't always something illegal or immoral. Your boy might not let you know if he's feeling lost, or different, or sad. I've treated many boys who have fallen into depression, and even some who have contemplated suicide.

And their parents had no idea.

I understand the feeling of desperation to figure out what the problem is. You want to solve it and make it go away.

Here's the bad news: you can't.

My guess is you already know that you can't, because you've tried. You've probably talked and talked and talked to your boy to the point where you are talking *at* your boy. He probably tells you everything is fine, if he says anything at all. Maybe you've taken it further and spoken to your son's teacher or a counselor at school, or even sent your child to see a counselor or therapist you found through your health insurance plan.

And maybe, if you're like most of the mothers I know, none of that has worked.

I'm here to tell you that you are not alone. There is a reason all the things you've tried haven't changed anything. I'm also here to tell you that there are things you can do that *will* work and that *will* set your son on the path to becoming the healthy, well-adjusted man you want him to grow up to be.

In other words, I'm here to help.

I come to you not only with professional expertise, but with a foundation of personal experience. My earliest memory is when I was around four years old. I remember covering my head in my bed in the middle of the night, trying to drown out the sound of my dad hitting my mother, crying until I fell asleep. At five the next morning, my mother, who now had two black eyes, woke me up and took me and my baby sister to my maternal grandparents' house. Then everyone went back to bed—except me. I stayed on the sofa by the door, crying.

A week later, we were back home, going on with our lives as if nothing ever happened.

This was not an isolated incident. The drinking and the violence, both against my mother and against me, continued.

My childhood experiences make me especially sensitive to recognize the danger signals and symptoms in the lives of the boys I see in my practice today.

In the following chapters I'll share what I've learned about adolescent boys in my 20-plus years of practice, as well as why the things you're doing now aren't making things any better. I'll also share some of the approaches and techniques I've learned and developed that do work, and why. And I'll explain what you, as your son's primary advocate, can do to help him get what he needs to grow up healthy and happy.

Finally, I'll introduce you to a group of young men who were once a lot like your son might be now, as well as the mothers and others who raised them. They'll share the stories of their experiences, what they learned, how they healed, and where they are today. Together, we'll show you that, despite what you might believe right now, your son's future is bright.

You only need the right tools to help him get there.

CHAPTER 1

Who Is Your Fantasy Son?

To get started on this journey and help you get the most out of this book, Let's begin with an exercise I use with the parents I see in my practice. It's designed to help them think about something they might never have considered before: the difference between their expectations for their son and the reality of who their son is. Those are usually two very different things.

Take a few minutes to complete the exercise. You'll need a piece of paper and a pen.

First, think about your fantasy son. By that I mean the child you saw in your mind when you first heard the words, "It's a boy." Who did you dream that boy would be today? A straight-A student? The captain of the football team? Class President? Would he have perfect manners? Would he always do what he was told?

Don't worry if this makes you feel uncomfortable, or even a little guilty. There really is no good or bad here. All parents naturally have dreams and expectations for their children, and you're not "wrong" for doing so.

Write all of those things down. You can easily fill at least half a page to a page.

Okay. Now comes the hard part.

Take that piece of paper, and everything it represents, and throw it away.

This might be painful, but it's important. Because as precious as he might be to you, the reality is that fantasy son does not exist. He could never have existed except in your imagination.

(But don't feel too bad. You probably aren't the parent your son fantasizes about, either!)

If you're feeling upset or emotional, that is completely normal. It's okay to grieve for the son you dreamed of raising and never had. You're letting go of something that is very close to your heart, even if it is only a fantasy. Take whatever time you need to process your feelings about letting go.

Okay.

Now take another piece of paper and write a new list, this time of things you know about the son you have today. Yes, there will be bad things, and you can and should include them. But I also want you to think about the good things. Maybe your son has a great sense of humor or a vivid imagination. Those things are important too.

Whatever you know about your son, write it all down. Again, try to fill at least a half a page.

You might notice that this new list is different from the first list you made. That is a good thing, because while that first list was not worth much, this new list can help you and your son move forward.

For example, when you look at what you've written on this list, you'll remember not to be surprised by your son's problem behavior. You've acknowledged and identified it, so you can now see where you need to set boundaries and develop solutions that will encourage your son to respect those boundaries.

You will also see some good qualities on your list. If you were unable to think of anything positive while you were writing things down, go back to your list until you come up with at least three positive things—no matter how angry or disappointed you feel right now.

This is critical, because these are the qualities you want and need to recognize when dealing with your child. If you are going to help him, you first need to show support and appreciation for the person he is, so you can build that person up.

This exercise is designed to bring you into the present moment. By letting go and grieving the fantasy son, you can stop trying to force your child to conform to an idea you invented years ago, before you knew what parenting was all about. Now, you can see your son for the person he truly is and discover what you can do to help him grow and thrive.

In other words, It's time to stop dreaming about who you wish your son could be and help him become the healthy, happy, and successful man he's supposed to be.

Let's get started.

CHAPTER 2

The State of Boyhood

S o, how DO we begin to build your son into a man who is healthy, happy and responsible? To begin, we need to understand the world your son is growing up in right now. And if your son is having trouble, I would be willing to bet that he is growing up without a dad.

There's a wound most troubled boys share, which, at its core, comes from the feeling that they don't have their father's unconditional love. This affects boys whose fathers are missing from their lives because of divorce or abandonment. It happens with boys who are victims of abuse. It even happens with boys who live in two-parent households and see their fathers nearly every day.

I call this phenomenon the "Absent Father."

The vast majority of the boys I see in my practice are growing up in homes where the father does not physically live in the home with them. These boys are being raised by single mothers. This isn't *always* the case, but we'll get to other situations later.

If you're a single mother, you don't need me to tell you how hard that is. Without a partner to help with child-rearing duties, most of the single moms I know feel like they have to fill both the role of father and the role of mother for their children. There aren't enough hours in the day for them to fill either role well, especially if there are other kids in the house who also need time and attention. Most single moms work outside the home to make sure their children have a roof over their head, food on the table, and clothes to wear. The rest of the time they're preparing food, cleaning up, making sure the kids do their homework, and driving to sports practices, teacher conferences, games, and activities.

It's overwhelming.

No wonder so many single moms feel frazzled and at the end of their ropes. If a child is having problems in school or with friends or even with the law, there's no extra energy to deal with that.

If that sounds like your experience, you are not alone. According to estimates, one in three boys currently lives in a home without a father or other strong male role model. The result is a crisis, and it's currently affecting a large number of America's boys.

According to most studies on the subject, boys who grow up without fathers grow up at a disadvantage. The simple fact that their father doesn't live with them makes them more likely than the rest of their peers to drop out of school, get involved in gangs, have trouble with the law, and experiment with drugs and alcohol.

I know this is true, not only from my research, but from my personal experience. I see it in my practice all the time, since the majority of the boys I work with come from divorced families. You may see some (or all) of those behaviors in your own son right now.

Studies also show that boys who grow up without fathers are dramatically more likely to get into serious trouble. For example:

- 70% of adolescent boys in residential treatment centers are fatherless.
- 72% of juveniles in state reform institutions grew up without parents or in single-parent homes.
- 72% of adolescent murderers grew up without fathers.

And most shockingly,

- More than 75% of all crime in America is committed by men who were fatherless as children.

I realize this is hard to hear if you're a single mother. You're no doubt trying to do the best you can, and hearing that your son is predisposed to a harder life simply because you don't share a home with his father is bound to be discouraging.

The good news is you are taking action right now. You wouldn't be reading this if you were willing to sit back and let things happen. You are already taking the first step to help your son while he's still a boy. You've just improved the odds for your son.

If you're not one of the many mothers who is raising her son alone, that doesn't necessarily mean he is benefiting from the advantage of having Dad in the house. A father doesn't have to live apart from his son to qualify as an "Absent Father." I work with several mothers who have a partner living with them at home in a relatively stable relationship who *still* feel like they're doing most of the parenting on their own. And that's not just a feeling—they are one hundred percent right.

That's why so many married or partnered mothers live lives that aren't so different from some single mothers. In many families the father is physically present, living in the home with his son, but for whatever reason his mind and his energy are elsewhere. These men have mentally checked out, and their boys (and their partners) suffer for it.

One common form this takes is the father who never grew up. These are the "fun" dads who want to be their son's buddy, who seem to always be available to take their boys out four-wheeling or fishing or golfing or on a trip to

Disneyland. They spend hours playing video games or watching football with their sons. This is a good thing. These boys have relationships with their fathers. The problem is, the father in those relationships is more like an older brother or a fun uncle.

When it comes to making sure that homework gets done or confronting their son about the bag of marijuana Mom found in his sock drawer or any of those parenting tasks that aren't "fun," this type of father is nowhere to be seen. All the hard work falls to Mom.

When it comes to the hard, painful, real work of parenting, the "fun" dad is absent.

Any father, even one who is not an addict or an abuser, can be physically present without being there in the way it counts—to provide the support, guidance, and discipline a boy needs to grow up healthy and well-adjusted. And while some of these fathers are absent for obvious reasons, like alcoholism or drug addiction, there are also dads who suffer from addictions that are easier to hide, like gambling or internet pornography. I've seen fathers who have mentally checked out due to depression or other mental health issues and some who are unable to participate in their sons' lives because of physical illness.

Any of these issues can prevent a father who is physically present in the home from being mentally and emotionally present to fulfill his role as a parent.

Believe it or not, a father can even be absent in one of those "perfect" TV sitcom-style families where everything looks normal on the surface. I term those "Emotionally Absent Fathers." They tend to be workaholic, perfectionist types who are too busy, stressed out, and wrapped up in their own lives and problems to take the time to provide the hands-on guidance their sons need. They feel fine leaving the "parenting" to Mom. They see it as "her job."

You don't have to be a single mom for your son to be growing up with an Absent Father. Even a dad who appears to be the perfect father to the rest of the world can be just as "absent" as a divorced or separated dad.

Unfortunately, that means his son will suffer similar consequences.

Another reality on the home front, besides the growing phenomenon of Absent Fathers, is the fact that most mothers *and* fathers work outside the home. Most of the boys I see in my practice, not to mention most boys in general, are coming home to an empty house. There's no mom (or dad) at home to welcome them back from school with milk and cookies and assistance with their homework. Instead, these kids' parenting is primarily performed by the internet or a video game or their cell phone. Except for the advanced technology, it's a lot like it was for boys back in the 1960s and '70s, when kids used to come home from school and spend the entire afternoon in front of the TV or talking on the phone with their buddies.

Later, when the parents finally do get home from work, they're stressed from the commute, they're tired from working all day, there's dinner to be made and a list of priorities they see as more important than Quality Time with the Kids. So it's, "Go do your homework or go play video games while I make dinner or catch up on what I need or want to do."

This is understandable. As I said before, there aren't enough hours in the day to be the parent you want to be.

But maybe you are one of the lucky few parents who can be home during the day, or maybe you manage to rally enough energy after work to engage with your son on a meaningful level. Even that is not always enough. Your son probably has a friend (or two) whose parents aren't around or who aren't as engaged, so the child is basically left to his own devices and allowed to do whatever he wants. That's likely where your son hangs out after school and on the weekends, instead of at home. On that turf he may be playing *Call of Duty* and using drugs or drinking or smoking or engaging in other risky behavior.

And what goes on when your son is at home? If you're like the mothers I work with, you fight with him about everything from unfinished homework to something as basic as sleep. Many adolescent boys don't get the sleep they need to function properly. They stay up late at night watching TV or playing video games or texting on their phones. As much as you'd like to make sure your son goes to bed, you're probably too tired. *You* need to go to bed!

So, you do, and he doesn't. He stays up until all hours playing games or virtually chatting or whatever he likes to do at night. The next morning when you're getting ready for work, what do you hear? "Mom, I'm too tired to go to school, can I stay home?"

You want him to do what he's supposed to do, which is get up and go to school. You *need* him to do what he's supposed to do. You don't have time to deal with this. You have to get yourself ready and out the door so you're not late for work. So, of course, you're the bad guy for nagging your poor, exhausted child.

But what else can you do?

Please understand that everything I'm saying here is a generalization. This is a basic overview of what the situation is like for most of the boys I work with. I know from professional experience that every family is unique, and that includes yours. But these are the most common things I see in my practice and in life, every day. Chances are good that you're seeing at least some of this in your son and in your home.

Another issue to consider is that home and family aren't the only major influencers your son is exposed to. What kind of support is he getting out in the world? What is the community around you doing to aid your son's journey from childhood to manhood?

The second biggest influence in your son's life after his family is school. We trust schools to teach our kids what they need to know to grow up to be solid, productive adults. But lately, not *all* of the kids at school have been receiving the same level of attention.

Ever since Title IX was passed in 1972, the majority of schools have focused more and more attention on girls. It started with simple things, like giving girls equal access and opportunity to play sports, but over the years it seems to have reached a fever pitch. It's all over the media constantly. Girls aren't doing enough science, so we need to encourage them to do more science. Girls aren't doing enough math, so we need to encourage them to get into math. Why aren't women's sports as popular as men's sports? We need to focus on girls' abilities instead of their looks. And on and on and on.

There's nothing wrong with boosting girls. For too long girls were left behind, and now they're getting their due. The problem is, with all of this focus on females, our boys have been forgotten. Nobody's talking about what boys need to succeed.

As a result, the boys are being left behind.

The statistics are alarming. Boys do as well as or better than girls on standard-ized tests. That means that their abilities and intelligence are essentially equal. However, according to researchers including *New York Times* opinion writer Christina Hoff Sommers (author of *The Boys at the Back)* and Michael Gurian (author of *The Minds of Boys),* equal potential has not been translating into equal performance.

Specifically, boys:

- have significantly higher rates of learning disabilities

- receive up to 70% of all Ds and Fs given to all students

- create 90% of all classroom discipline problems

Boys also have lower grade point averages than girls, and they are more likely to drop out of high school and less likely to graduate than their female counterparts.

Why is this happening? Why are our schools failing to serve our boys better?

Maybe it's because the vast majority of teachers are female, and they relate more to a female mindset. Or maybe because, as students, girls are more traditionally "likeable." They don't talk back. They don't misbehave. They're usually more focused on what they're supposed to be doing. Not because they're "better," but because they're wired differently. It's a matter of biology.

This brings me to another not exactly surprising fact about boys. Five out of six children who are sent to see the doctor for ADD or ADHD are, in fact, boys.

Since children are usually referred to specialists by their teachers, this indicates that today's teachers don't like what they're seeing from the boys in their classes. And they're sending them to doctors to get them to behave more like the girls do.

As I said before, this is not biologically possible. Boys and girls are wired differently.

If I were a student today, I probably would be one of those boys who is sent to see the doctor for ADD or ADHD medication. It's not that I was unintelligent, or that I didn't try—I simply couldn't concentrate. Every time I tried to sit down and read, intrusive thoughts would invade my mind and interrupt whatever I tried to focus on. I did everything I could to distract myself from those thoughts, but this also distracted me from what I was supposed to be doing in the first place. So it didn't get done.

Maybe you've seen similar behavior from your son. Maybe his teachers have complained about it.

As a psychotherapist I've studied ADD and ADHD, and I know now that I was actually experiencing post-traumatic stress disorder (PTSD)—the same thing soldiers suffer when they return from a war. In my case, the PTSD was a result of severe abuse I experienced during my own childhood, but I have seen the same behaviors in many of the boys I work with who have been diagnosed with ADD or ADHD.

Abuse isn't the only factor that can lead to PTSD in a child. Common, "normal" things like parents splitting up, being bullied, or being rejected by peers can haunt kids for years. PTSD can also result from what we call "vicarious traumatization," which happens when a child hears details of a family member or close person being abused or hurt. Kids can even get PTSD from something they see on TV or in a movie. They play out the disturbing scene in their head over and over again as if it happened in real life.

This is why I don't advocate telling kids "brutally" honest details or letting them watch TV that is beyond their maturity level. You're not being mean when you won't let your child watch *The Walking Dead*. It actually is for his own good.

Of course, there are teachers who enjoy working with boys and understand what makes them tick and how to get the most out of them. But a teacher can do damage if she's too soft and mothering and lets a male student get away with things he shouldn't. I can't tell you how many mothers complain to me about their son's teacher, saying, "I'm tired of her telling me what a sweetheart my son is!"

Again, what I'm saying here is general. Every boy is different, every teacher is different, and of course, every case is different. But from a purely statistical standpoint, the way our schools are educating our boys is having a negative effect. Today, not only are more girls going on to college than boys, more of them are also graduating, and more are going on to earn advanced degrees.

And the boys? Now they're the ones falling behind in math and science.

What that means is that whatever inequality (real or perceived) our education system was trying to correct back in the 1970s has now been overcorrected. Today, it's our boys who need special attention.

And, for the most part, they're just not getting it.

What You Should Know about ADD and ADHD Medications

I believe that ADD and ADHD are over-diagnosed today, and that medications, especially ADD and ADHD medications, are over-used when it comes to treating boys with behavioral problems. I have worked with hundreds of school-age boys during my years in practice, and the majority of them walked into my office under the influence of at least one ADD or ADHD drug, if not some combination of drugs. You will meet some of those boys in the Case Studies section of this book.

Working with those boys and others like them, I discovered that most of the behaviors typically associated with ADD and ADHD can be linked to other factors, ranging from depression to PTSD (post-traumatic stress disorder) to environmental factors like instability. When that underlying cause is treated and dealt with, the ADD or ADHD symptoms often disappear. Medications, on the other hand, treat only the symptoms (the behavior), though often not effectively and almost never without side effects.

Even so, if your son is having problems, especially in school, chances are good that his counselor will suggest you talk to the boy's doctor. The doctor will then diagnose him with ADD or ADHD and send you to the pharmacy with a prescription.

The fault is not entirely your doctor's. If you go to a doctor with a problem, whether that problem is allergies or headaches or depression, he or she will look for a medical solution, and thanks to the wonders of modern science, that solution most frequently comes in the form of a pill. Medications are the primary tools in a physician's arsenal, especially when it comes to ADD and ADHD. After all, your medical doctor hasn't been trained to analyze your son's behavior over time or to understand the causes of that behavior. Medical doctors are not specifically trained to help boys modify behavior or cope with personal challenges. A pill seems like the best and easiest option available.

But it's not necessarily the healthiest or most effective option for your son.

Many parents think of a doctor's prescription as a "magic bullet" that will automatically make their child's symptoms disappear. In fact, medication only works on about fifty percent of ADHD cases. Most drugs have side effects, and the kids who take the drugs suffer the effects. If you've ever paid attention to one of the myriad of prescription drug commercials on television, you've heard the long list of unpleasant possibilities the drug company is legally required to disclose. ADD and ADHD medications are no exception.

What side effects might your son experience if he takes ADD or ADHD drugs? In his book, *The ADD Answer: How to Help Your Child Now,* Dr. Frank Lawlis lists the most common side effects for ADHD medications:

- Nervousness
- Insomnia
- Confusion
- Depression
- Agitation
- Irritability
- Stunted growth and development

He also lists less-common side effects including:

- Hyperactivity
- Hypersensitivity (allergy-type reactions to environmental agents)
- Anorexia
- Nausea
- Dizziness
- Heart palpitations
- Headaches
- Dyskinesia (movement-of-the-body problems)
- Drowsiness
- Hypertension (high blood pressure)

- Tachycardia (rapid, racing heartbeat)

- Angina (heart pain)

- Arrhythmia (heart rate changes)

- Abdominal pain

- Lowered threshold for seizures

As long as this list is, it doesn't take into account the risks associated with taking these drugs for an extended period of time, including the possibility of psychosis and liver damage. When you consider the fact that medication is effective only in about fifty percent of ADHD cases, you see how that magnifies the risk even more.

These specific side effects will not necessarily happen to your son, and I am not advising you to simply ignore your doctor's advice. Sometimes medication truly is the best solution. But unless you know that your child's case is extreme enough to merit medication, I suggest that you consider a doctor's ADD or ADHD diagnosis as just one piece of the puzzle for helping your son. Before you start him on an ADD or ADHD medication, ask his doctor or psychiatrist to refer you to a therapist in your area who specializes in working with boys like yours to explore possible non-medical solutions. Enroll your son in a group program like The Quest Project® where he will have a chance to actively work through his issues and channel his energy constructively.

There are multiple options. Consider which is best for you and your son.

The one place where boys do generally get the type of support they need is the world of sports. Most sports teams are divided by gender, especially once children reach their preteen years. That gives boys a chance to interact and excel and learn to work together in a male-dominated environment. Usually the coach is a male who understands what is and isn't appropriate in terms of risk-taking and aggression, and who has at least some experience dealing with the anger, disappointment, and other emotional issues that come with playing the game. Good coaches model positive behavior and provide boundaries, encouragement, and praise, all of which help boys mature into healthy, well-adjusted men. Engaging in sports helps boys expend some of their boundless energy—a win for them and a win for you!

Still, the wide world of sports is not a perfect world. Not every coach is a "good man," and many coaches are women. Not all coaches are adept at dealing with boys in general, or at handling the challenges sports present. Some coaches are not concerned with their players' success off the field or court. They don't focus on their players' grades, their social skills, or their development into healthy, confident, capable young men. Some coaches care more about winning (and the bragging rights that come with it). Coaches are, after all, only human. Some coaches cross boundaries and break rules to maintain (or gain) an advantage. Some coaches don't pay attention to the needs of their players beyond the need to win.

A coach's expectation may directly contradict the parents' expectations for their sons.

That's sports, and that's life. But the support and life lessons, the opportunity to bond and test themselves, and the engagement for fun that sports offers are usually well worth any negative aspects. Sports gave me something positive to focus on and work toward when I was a boy.

That's equally true for a lot of boys today.

Non-school institutions do not fare as well when it comes to helping our boys become men. Many of us grew up with the guidelines and standards and community provided by organized religion. But how effective were those institutions in teaching us how to be an adult? Church was a non-factor in my growing up—and I grew up in the Bible Belt!

From what I've seen, today's religious institutions don't play a solid role in guiding young boys into manhood. Part of this is because religion is less important in most people's everyday lives today than it was some generations ago. I'm talking about overall statistics. It may not look that way where you live, but the percentage of Americans who call themselves religious has dropped over the years. Even in the Bible Belt, for every ten boys who come in to my office, maybe one is involved in religious activities.

Even for those boys, religious institutions and activities aren't providing much in the way of practical guidance for growing into a good man. Coming-of-age rituals like Catholic Confirmation and the Jewish Bar Mitzvah are more about the ceremony than they are about teaching, testing, or challenging boys in a way that guides them into adulthood. There are classes to attend and things to learn and remember, but the boys don't feel any more "grown up" when they're finished than when they began—because they are not. The world doesn't see or treat them any differently.

The Boy Scouts provide a similar experience wrapped up in a secular package. Scouts earn badges for learning new skills and accomplishing specific tasks, like tying knots and building fires. In Scouts, boys often accomplish these things with the help of their parents. Since Dad's not around in so many cases, that leaves Mom as the helper. That strips "manly" from the scouting activities.

While weeding the vegetable beds at the community garden with Mom is good and helpful, it doesn't teach a boy much about being a man.

Ultimately, the badges boys earn don't mean a lot because they're not about the transition to manhood. Boys don't change in any significant way to earn them. As with religious ceremonies, nothing happens that *transforms* them.

Thus, in the absence of any real institutional support, or any feeling of being a part of something bigger or more meaningful, most boys will seek validation from the one institution that's always there. That would be their peer group.

Yes—other boys.

As I mentioned before, boys usually hang out at the house of that one kid who has the least supervision at home. One boy in the crowd will emerge as a leader, usually the boy who's a little more street smart, who's already done some experimenting and knows what he can get away with and how to get away with it.

That boy will encourage the other boys, take them under his wing, and "parent" them in his own way. He'll say, "Hey, Jimmy, you're quick. You're good at being quick. So, we'll steal this thing because you're so quick."

And if Jimmy craves validation or challenge in his life, or if he desperately wants to prove himself and impress somebody, well, you can see where this leads.

Especially if you're Jimmy's Mom.

Maybe you know where it leads from personal experience. Or maybe you're seeing signs of something in your son that makes you nervous. Maybe you worry he's heading down the wrong path, and you've realized that you can't count on your son's school or any extracurricular institution like religion or scouting to provide him the guidance he needs to become the man he's meant to be.

This brings me to the biggest issue your son faces right now: **If he doesn't get help while he's still a boy, he will almost certainly carry the problems he's having with him and grow into a troubled man.**

Growing up doesn't automatically heal the wounds of childhood. If anything, the pressures of adulthood can make those wounds more painful and powerful and the consequences even more detrimental to a full and successful life.

So what can you do to help your son?

I'm about to show you.

CHAPTER 3

What's Missing

W e've looked closely at how your son sees the world right now, and we've recognized what his world fails to provide for him. This is good to know, but now what?

To help your son get the things you haven't been able to give him at home and the things he's not getting from the institutions in your community, you first need to understand exactly what he needs and what he's not getting.

Mothers I meet in my practice already feel like they're bending over backwards giving their all to help their boy. And it's still not working!

If this is true for you, understand that it's not your fault. You are not failing your son.

The problem is basic biology.

At its most basic level, the transition from boyhood to manhood is about a boy breaking *away* from his mother and learning to stand on his own two feet. He's looking for answers to questions like, "Who is the man I'm going to become?" and, "Who's around that can give me that example or model?"

As much as you love your son, those are answers you cannot provide.

Part of what makes parenting an adolescent so challenging is that at the same time your son is feeling drawn to this new world of men, he is still terrified to leave your side. The first and biggest challenge boys face as they grow up is separating from Mom. Who can blame your son for feeling attached to the safety and comfort of being cared for and feeling loved? Even when he's acting like a complete jerk, he still doesn't want to let go of you. In fact, that may be *why* your son is acting like a complete jerk.

Boys test their mothers. On one hand they want to see how far they can push the boundaries; on the other hand they want to run back to Mom's side and be safe.

In an ideal world, this is where Dad steps in and says, "No, wait a minute. You're not going to hide, you're not running back to Mom, and you're going to feel this." Because when a boy pushes past his fear and faces it, that's where the growth happens.

Because it's so challenging, this is where a lot of boys get stuck. One primary reason is the lack of a strong male role model to guide them. The current epidemic of Absent Fathers means too many boys have no one to tell them, "You can do it," and push them forward toward manhood.

And yes, this includes boys who have a father living at home.

You may be wondering why you, Mom, can't be the person to guide your son on this journey. After all, you've gotten him this far. You probably know him better than anyone. But even when you say those exact same words, you get a very different reaction than when the words come from Dad. When Dad nudges your son away from you and out into the world, it's empowering. When you nudge your son away from you, he may feel rejected. He may feel you're no longer there to run back to. This is both painful and scary to a boy who is still unsure of his place in the world.

The other problem when you assume this role is that without a father or other male mentor to guide him, your son is still biologically hard-wired to seek out a man to help him through the transition. With no father or other adult male stepping in, the easiest place for him to find that mentor is in his peer group, and that can be trouble. Most adolescent boys don't understand what manhood means. They think proving they're men requires taking crazy risks to demonstrate bravery, and that behavior is encouraged and rewarded. (A great example of this is portrayed in the book *Lord of the Flies*.)

Adolescent boys don't understand that becoming a man, at its core, means stepping up and accepting responsibility. They don't even know what that means.

Adolescents are fresh human beings. The weird feelings and changes they experience are new, they're scary, and they're painful. No wonder your son wants you to keep taking care of him, just as you always have. The unknown is frightening, especially if there's no one ahead of him showing him the ropes and letting him know that what he's feeling is normal and surmountable and that he can do it.

Despite the pitfalls, a lot of boys make the transition to manhood without the support they need. As a consequence, more and more young men grow older without growing up. They lack the guidance of mentors to show them how to be responsible men. They don't learn what they need to know to function in the adult world.

The situation is not unique to this generation of young men. Those perpetual adolescents I mentioned in the last chapter? There's a good chance that, when they were teenagers, no one taught them how to be men either.

The failure of adult males to mature is more pronounced now than ever, but the problem has been building for generations. We see fathers scream at each other on the Little League diamond. We see our leaders scream at each other on the Senate floor. We're looking at a bunch of—and this is not a clinical term—adult babies. Our world is being run by two or three generations of men who grew up without learning the skills adult men need. They are losing pieces of themselves and of what it means to be a man.

Our boys are the latest casualty of this phenomenon.

The change has been gradual, over decades. It started with the Industrial Revolution, picked up speed after World War II, and has continued to worsen decade by decade. The initial reason for the change was economic. Our society changed from a predominantly agrarian economy, where most people lived and worked on farms or in small communities, to an industrial economy, where more people live in cities. In the industrial economy, people tend to leave their home and family, and sometimes their hometown and support systems, to work in factories and office buildings.

Over the years more and more men have made this move away from the farm and the shop into factories and offices to earn their living. Prior to industrialization, boys grew up working alongside their fathers, as well as their uncles, brothers, and neighbors, on the farm and in the shop. They learned how to be men by growing up with other men.

Today our boys have only each other to learn from. They don't have the benefit of observing and interacting with other men to see what it means to be a man. They don't see or experience how men work and relax and interact with other people. They don't see how men handle stress and adversity and conflict. They miss the pivotal experience of learning at their father's knee, being given tasks to accomplish, and feeling the pride and sense of responsibility boys once earned by learning and completing those tasks. That's what "growing up" used to be.

In our present society we find happiness in having material things rather than in accomplishing things. The transition between childhood and adulthood used to entail significant accomplishment. Both boys and girls learned to do specific tasks and accomplish things that made a difference. Once they did, they moved on to the next, bigger challenge. Growing into an adult involved learning how to be useful and how to be productive, one step at a time.

The general consensus is that without those challenges our boys have it easy. There's talk of "entitlement" and how this generation of boys *and* girls feels they deserve more than they earn. But by failing to teach our boys real-life skills or hold them accountable for their actions, we are not making their lives easier—especially not in the long term. What do they gain from hiding out in the basement smoking pot and playing video games instead of having a job? They miss learning how to interact with a boss, to get along with co-workers, to accomplish assigned tasks, to take criticism, to handle money. Without those skills they will find it hard to take care of themselves and function in the adult world.

When boys don't learn *how* to grow up, they simply don't grow up. They stay stuck in adolescence.

How can you make sure this doesn't happen to your son? What can you do to ensure your son gets what he needs, not only to grow older, but to grow up healthy, happy, and responsible?

Five things are critical for a boy's transition into manhood. Here's a list, with some tips to help you see that he receives them.

1. Your boy needs a mentor.

While it may sound sexist, I believe it's true that only a man can show a boy what manhood means. Whether your son's father is a part of his life or not, your son needs to spend time with an adult male mentor who is ready, willing, and able to provide the encouragement and example he needs.

How much time? According to my research, an adolescent boy should be spending a minimum of three to five hours a week, every week, with a male role model who provides guidance, answers his questions, and engages in his life to show that he cares.

If your son's father is already playing that role, ideally he can and will make the time commitment to guide your son through this transition. As for the quality of that time, you might gently suggest he read this book for an idea of the type of support your son needs. Playing *Call of Duty* has its place, but right now your child needs boundaries and guidance.

If turning to your son's father is not an option, or if he isn't the right man for the job, look to the community around you. You'd be surprised how many men in your circle would be willing and even honored to be a regular part of your son's life—an uncle, a family friend, a neighbor, a teacher, or a coach. You know your son best, you know what he likes, you know who he feels connected to and comfortable with. The ideal mentor is someone whom you and your son both trust, who knows and likes your son, and who is happily available to spend time to help him grow.

2. Your boy needs a safe place to deal with his pain.

Every adolescent experiences pain. It's an essential part of growing up. However, if you're like most mothers, when you see your boy in pain, your primary impulse is to do whatever you can to make that pain go away. No one likes to see someone they love suffer.

But the pain of growing up is different. You can't make it go away, nor should you try. While the pain of growing up is not pleasant for your son, it serves a purpose in helping him stretch beyond the little boy he is and grow into a fully functional adult.

It isn't easy. You've heard the term "growing pains"—this is it.

This type of pain is so normal and natural, it's a major reason even boys from perfectly intact and functional families join my program. Even for boys whose fathers live under the same roof, whose families are supportive and do everything "right," the confusion of adolescence and of breaking away from Mom just plain hurts.

If, like the majority of the boys I work with, your son doesn't feel loved and accepted unconditionally by his father, those growing pains have an extra dimension. However, even that pain can be processed and dealt with in a healthy, constructive way, especially if your son has a mentor helping him through the rough patches.

At this point you might be thinking, "Wait a minute. I was a teenager once. I remember those years were pretty horrible, at least a lot of the time. Isn't the pain you're talking about a normal part of growing up?"

Yes, as I said, this pain is normal. But the fact that it's normal doesn't mean you should ignore it and wait for it to go away. Many children can manage the ups and downs of adolescence on their own, but not every child has the tools to deal with pain effectively. Those children find ways of coping that can ultimately damage them.

For example, if your son is using alcohol or drugs, he probably thinks he is relaxing or partying or maybe rebelling against your rules. But substance abuse is a form of what mental health professionals call "self-medicating." Substances like alcohol and drugs numb pain. Those numbing qualities are what make them so much fun and feel so good to use. But in the long run, numbing the pain does not make it go away. Instead, it may set up your son for a lifetime of needing to numb any pain he encounters.

Almost any addictive behavior, from drinking and drugs to dependence on sex, pornography, gambling, and even food, has its roots in the inability to deal with pain. Your job at this point is not to make your son's pain go away, but neither is your job to ignore it. Help him experience it and work through it by giving him a safe space to feel and process his feelings.

Let him know you understand he's having a hard time, that it's normal, and that you trust he can get through it. Make it clear that if he needs help dealing with his feelings, you are there for him by supporting him or finding a place for him to process those feelings. Do not try to fix it by saying: "It will be ok," or "Don't feel that way," or by redirecting his attention. Those are all messages that something is wrong. In fact, nothing is wrong or the matter. He is feeling, which is normal. This can be extremely hard for moms to understand, especially since they have tried to fix all their sons' hurts in the past.

Working through his pain will be one of the most important challenges in your son's journey to adulthood. For most boys, growing pains are a given. It's crucial that your son feels safe acknowledging that pain, and that he has the space he needs to deal with it, so he can move past it and not carry childhood wounds (and the behaviors they might spark) into his adult life.

Offering a safe place to deal with pain is a critical part of helping a boy grow up healthy and whole.

3. Your boy needs the support of a community.

I mentioned community earlier in this chapter—the friends, relatives, coaches, and teachers who are already a part of your son's world. That same community can play an active and specific role in your son's transition to manhood.

Hundreds of years ago the growing up of boys was a community responsibility. In many societies around the globe, and in some native cultures here in the

United States, that is still the case. Boys are guided on their path to manhood by the male elders in their community, often with special transition periods separating the adolescent boys from their mothers and leading them through a series of tasks and experiences designed to help them find their identities and learn responsible behavior.

These initiation rituals sometimes include a spiritual component, and they usually focus on a challenge the boy must complete. Completion instills confidence. The community celebrates, symbolically welcoming the boy into the world of men.

Unfortunately, these opportunities for our boys are few and far between. Churches, synagogues, Boy Scout troops, and other organizations offer marks of passage into adulthood, but as I mentioned previously, these rituals are more about the ceremony itself than they are about boys changing in any meaningful way. They are largely symbolic and lack meaning in the context of the larger community, at least as far as society recognizing the transition from boyhood to manhood.

Employ your community to provide a support network for your son, even if it's informal. Whether or not your son's father is his primary mentor, there is a place for the wisdom of men who are Not Dad and who know Things Dad Doesn't Know. Every man has a different way of seeing the world, different skills to share, and different experiences. Each unique baseline provides a different perspective and different feedback. Your son may have more in common with one of these men than he does with his own father.

Regardless, the more healthy men your son is regularly exposed to and the more of these men he knows and trusts, the better access he will have to quality support. He'll have more opportunities to connect with people he relates to, who understand him, and who give him that spark of insight he needs to make the transition to manhood easier and more meaningful.

Community not only helps ease the transition, it also pushes your son through the difficult spots and acknowledges and celebrates his successful passage. The community witnesses the process of your son's learning, changing, and maturing, and because they've witnessed it, they recognize that he is a different person. They witness your son's experience and empower him by saying, "You did it. You're a man now."

Your boy's experience is meaningful and profound.

4. Your boy needs a ritual to mark his transformation.

You may not want to take your son into the wilderness and have him build a fire or kill a deer to prove he's a man. That doesn't mean you need to let him become an adult without some acknowledgment that he's growing and changing and leaving behind the boy he was. Your son needs validation that he is different, that he is progressing on a worthy path, and that he is growing up. Ritual provides that validation.

Ritual doesn't need to be elaborate or formal. It can be a simple conversation. Ritual is taking the time away from the everyday to mark your son's transition. It's putting voice to it, saying, "I know this is the beginning of a change for you, and that you're no longer a little boy, and I want you to know that I can identify it and I can see it." Noticing the little things that indicate big changes, and letting your son know that you see them is a powerful ritual.

When your son faces a challenge, assure him: "I'm going to find out what you need" or, "I'm going to work as hard as I can to meet your needs. You don't have to understand every word I'm saying, just understand that I know you're in transition." Even if he rolls his eyes at you (which he very well might), what matters is that he knows you validate what he's going through. He will feel good knowing that you're aware, that you understand, and that you are there for him.

Even if he acts like you're crazy.

5. Your boy needs a sense of achievement, importance and change.

Your role in your son's transition is fundamentally about communication. When your son does well, when you see him growing and changing and accomplishing things, he needs to know you notice. He needs your encouragement. If he does well and no one notices, what's the point? Change means nothing to your son if no one acknowledges it—if *you* don't acknowledge it.

The flipside is that, as important as it is to acknowledge and validate when your son does well, it's equally important to avoid telling your son what you *don't* want him to do or be. I call these "don't be" messages. When you continually focus on what he does wrong, it sends a message that he makes mistakes, that mistakes are not okay, that he's not good enough, and that he will never be good enough. That sets him up for a lifetime of depression.

When a boy feels as if no one cares about him or as if he will never amount to anything, he truly believes it doesn't matter what he does. He can even believe that he, as a human being, does not matter. This belief leads to risky behavior, especially as he moves into adolescence.

Rather than focus on the behavior you don't want to see, focus on what your son is doing right. Build up from there. When you catch him meeting and exceeding your expectations, let him know you notice. That builds a healthy foundation for continued achievement.

Slow, steady achievement is what your son needs to make a healthy transition to manhood.

When to Contact the Authorities

After nearly two decades in the mental health field, I know that nothing is more painful and difficult for parents than contacting the authorities to help with an out-of-control child. No one wants to involve the police or mental health officials when they're dealing with a problem with their son. They don't want to appear paranoid or overly dramatic. They don't want to admit to the world that they've "failed" to control their child or to raise him properly. They worry about the long-term consequences of alerting the police or mental hospital. Will their child have a record? Will other people find out? How will it affect his future?

These are genuine reasons for concern, but none of it matters if you fear that your child is a danger to himself or others. Safety is your first priority.

If your child is suicidal or homicidal, get help immediately. Your primary goal is to do what it takes to ensure your son's safety and the safety of those around him. If there is immediate danger, don't wait. Call 911 or take him to the hospital yourself.

If danger is not immediate but your son's behavior is beyond your control, there are still questions you need to ask yourself and steps you may need to take to temper the situation. This is especially important if your son's behavior makes you feel threatened. If your son is aggressive towards you, don't let it slide. As the person who has been the authority for your son since the day he was born—you wiped his rear end and dried his tears and tucked him into bed at night—you might still think, "I'm bigger than he is, I can take him down if I have to." But the day comes when you stand eye-to-eye with that same child you used to lift over your head, and now he's pushing back. For the first time ever, you feel afraid of your own son.

The truth is simple: If it ever, ever reaches a point where you feel threatened, it's gone too far. When your son violates your personal space, that's the beginning of domestic violence. You won't handle it with a yelling match. You will lose. This is a male whose testosterone is pumping, and he will outdo you. Your son needs to understand that violence is never okay to resolve family conflicts. I recommend that the first step to deal with your boy's problem behavior entails "natural consequences." If your son breaks rules that you have established, he makes a choice that leads to a pre-determined consequence that you both know about. His inappropriate behavior amounts to his choosing not to have what he normally enjoys.

This is how it works. Your son wants something (as boys always do). You want something (you want your son to learn something or do/not do something specific). You give him the option that he can have what he wants after he chooses and accomplishes his task. After he does his homework or chores (encouraged behaviors), he can play video games, talk on the phone, or watch TV. Once he stops yelling, cussing, or breaking things (discouraged behaviors), he can play video games, talk on the phone, or watch TV.

I suggest focusing on a maximum of three behaviors at a time. Once he has accomplished the first set of appropriate behaviors, move on to a new set of behaviors to encourage or discourage. (There is usually a learning curve which can take a few months.)

If this step doesn't work, explain to him, "If you keep up this behavior, we're taking it to the next level." That might mean a session with a counselor or, if he's already in counseling, exploring the possibility of an in-patient program.

If he still does not modify his behavior, I recommend one of the most difficult things I ever ask parents to do. But I promise, it works, and it can help you avoid bigger problems down the line.

Call your local police station and arrange to meet (without your son) with the "relationship officer." This is the policeman who actively represents his department in your community. Talk to that person about your son and the problems you are having. Tell him (a male is preferable in this situation) you might want him to have a "scared straight" conversation with your son.

Police are trained to diffuse difficult situations. They know how to say, "Listen son, you get in your mom's face, I'm going to come with the handcuffs and put you in the back of the car, and you will sit in a cell" in a way that boys take seriously. They know how to make the prospect of punishment feel very, very real. And while it sounds harsh or extreme, it's the very thing boys who are threatening violence need to hear.

In most cases, one visit from a police officer is enough to nip threatening behavior in the bud. However, if the behavior doesn't stop, it's important to follow through. Bring the officer back to do what he said he would do. Police officers usually have a plan to handle these situations. They will come to your house, go through the process, handcuff your son, and put him in the back of the police car. Instead of taking your son to the station, they are more likely to sit in the driveway and talk to him. At the end of the conversation, they will release your boy and tell him he's getting another chance.

This might sound harsh, and it may very well terrify your child. But in my experience, the best way to get ahead of a problem like this is to demonstrate that you are serious. This works better than repeated threats to call the police with no follow-through. In those cases, by the time a mother finally feels forced to call the police, her son almost automatically ends up in jail.

If you worry that your son is suicidal, act swiftly and decisively. If he's threatening to hurt himself, don't try to determine whether he's serious or just trying to get attention. Go straight to the hospital. If your child cuts himself, do the same thing.

It's my experience that boys use cutting to hold parents hostage. They tell their mothers, "I didn't really mean it" as a way of getting extra attention, and then their mothers bend over backwards to try to make things okay. However, as intuitive as it may seem to smother him with more love and attention, that's not what your son needs at that point.

When it comes to mental health, boys play games. You want to take away that option. The best way is to treat the incident seriously. Take him to the hospital for a 72-hour stay and evaluation. Make him understand that threatening suicide is serious, and that, as his parent, you are not going to risk letting that happen to your child.

Most parents I work with are terrified to have this conversation with a child who may be suicidal. They worry about making things worse. But if your son is threatening to harm himself, you need to lay out a specific plan and tell him, "These are the things that are going to get you better. We're going to try counseling. We're going to try in-patient treatment. If not in-patient, we'll do a residential program." By that point, if a boy is not serious about harming himself, talk of suicide usually ends. If it doesn't, you have already laid the groundwork for the next steps. All you need to do is follow through and get him the help he needs.

If as a result of these early interventions you realize your son would be best served by an in-patient program, know that sometimes an in-patient stay provides the exact type of reset a boy needs to get past his problems and make a fresh start. The key is finding the right program to help your son. I recommend you research options as soon as you think your son might be a candidate for a residential program. Get referrals from doctors, counselors, and parents whose boys have gone through it. Educate yourself as much as possible. Work with a counselor to set up a plan. And don't forget to get some support for yourself. As a parent, you need counseling to coach you through the process and be sure you're doing the right thing for your son.

You don't have to do it alone.

CHAPTER 5

The Quest Project®

E very quest begins with a question. This was mine:

"Why are so many boys suffering, and what can be done to help them?"

The day I asked that question, I was alone in the wilderness on a Vision Quest. I had signed up for a men's retreat in the midst of my psychology studies, which coincided with my own healing journey to deal with the lingering effects of my difficult childhood.

Suddenly I found myself in the forest in the middle of the night looking for answers to questions that had plagued me since I was a boy, looking for what I missed growing up that left me wanting and wounded.

If I couldn't recoup those things, I could at least understand what they were and figure out how to become a whole person without them.

My goal was to stop making the same mistakes over and over again and to find a way to live the happy, healthy life I deserved. But a Vision Quest isn't only about healing old wounds. It also sparks a vision, and that vision can provide guidance for the journey ahead.

My *Vision* looked like this.

> *I am seeing the world from the moon. I see a gray mass moving toward me from the top of the earth, coming over the North Pole. I look closer and realize that the gray mass*

consists entirely of boys, and they are all headed to me for help.

I am the light they are moving towards—they want to escape the dark.

What did my vision tell me? First, that it wasn't all about me. There were a lot of boys who were wanting and wounded, just like I was. These boys were being abandoned physically, emotionally, in all shapes and forms.

I knew at that moment that I endured my difficult childhood for a reason—because I was put on this earth to reach those boys and help them.

I also knew that before I could help anyone else heal, I needed to heal myself. I needed to learn what specific things I missed in my growing up years. I needed to research and experiment how to fill those empty, hurting places inside of me. Essentially, I needed to become my own case study.

I believed that if I could heal myself, I could then apply the process to help other boys heal while they're still young. I believed I could help them avoid the pain and mistakes I had been dealing with for my entire adult life.

My vision of boys streaming toward me for help was the birth of The Quest Project®.

It didn't happen right away. For the first six months after my Vision Quest, I concentrated on my own healing and on my education, so that I would be ready to give the boys my all. I knew there was a lot of work to be done.

I also assisted on other Vision Quest weekends and, in the process, got to know a powerful man named Henry Thurman. With a group called the Pride Program in Wisconsin, Henry worked with gang members to give them an alternative to the streets. Henry impressed me. He reached these young men and made an impact. After watching him work, I felt brave enough to approach him with my idea:

"I want to get to young men sooner, instead of having to wait until they are adults. Why aren't we getting to them as teenagers?"

Henry was already working with boys in African-American communities in his area. I visited him and worked with him while I did my own research. Eventually he invited me to co-lead with him, and since my psychology background complemented his own training in education, he looked to me for opinions about his processes. Soon he began implementing my suggestions.

I had a glimpse of how my own vision might come to life.

I tried to get my own program going twice, once in 1996 and again in 1997, but quickly discovered that I was making the move too soon. I wasn't yet established as a therapist, I hadn't yet built a reputation for working with boys, and I lacked the experience to formulate an entire weekend retreat, staff it, and facilitate it. I decided to continue my research and work with patients one-on-one, knowing that I would try again when I was ready.

A few years later, I saw my opportunity. A local hospital sought a part-time therapist for their patient clinic. I took the job, got to know the directors, and eventually went to them with an idea: *What if I run a boys' group at the hospital?* The directors gave me the go-ahead, and I put together some of the processes I had developed into a makeshift program. I recruited a group of five boys to work with me, and we started meeting once a week.

Each process I used was based in psychological theory and the research I had done both in school and in the field. However, I had never before created a full program on my own, so I made a conscious decision to keep the process fluid. I wanted to be free to change things as I went along, to get rid of what didn't work, to expand on what did work, to move parts around, and to add new elements depending on how the boys progressed and what they needed next.

As the weeks went by, it became clear that the program worked. Parents raved about their sons' progress, and that was the success I had hoped for. I also realized that there were many more boys in my community beyond the hospital who could benefit from the same kind of experience.

After I took two groups of boys through the hospital program, it was time to launch The Quest Project®.

I still have the spiral notebook where I put the very first program together. I kept the once-a-week model because it had worked so well, and I sketched out a ten-week schedule designed to take a group of boys through a modern-day rite of passage, similar to the initiation rituals in ancient and native cultures that guided boys into manhood. It would have the community element, because it would revolve around a group of boys working together and supporting each other. It would include challenges for the boys to complete to gain a sense of accomplishment. And everything, including the challenges themselves, would be designed with a therapeutic purpose. I specifically developed every step of the program to help the boys uncover their pain, face it, and heal from it as they progressed from week to week. They would graduate transformed, stronger and healthier than before, and well on their way to becoming responsible men.

Once I had the plan on paper, I crafted a brochure to advertise it. Eight boys signed up right off the bat. I signed a lease on a new, bigger office space, and The Quest Project® was up and running.

My very first Quest Project® was a group of eight troubled boys who ranged from sixteen to eighteen years old. Teenagers. Right away, as one would expect with teenagers, someone stepped up to challenge me. This boy was eighteen, a rich kid with a sense of entitlement. He came to the program because he'd been in trouble for truancy, stealing, and generally acting out.

This kid—a young man—made it clear from the get-go that I was not going to get to him. He wasn't going to talk, he wasn't going to cooperate, he wasn't going to let me help him. He was too tough for that. (At least, that's how he wanted the other boys in the group to see him.)

It was a major challenge to face my first time out. But within the first week or so, I was able to reach him. Maybe because my intention was never to make him the problem or shame him or tell him he was a bad person who needed to change. I was there to help him, uplift him, and make his life better—to make all their lives better—because they weren't bad boys. I knew that they were wounded, and my goal was to help them heal so that they could live the kind of lives they deserved.

Once this boy understood my intentions, he stopped being a problem and emerged as a leader within the group that the rest of the boys followed throughout the ten weeks.

Another boy in my first group was sixteen. His dad and mom had divorced, his mother was outspoken, and he blamed his mother for driving his father away. He was so angry about the divorce that he wouldn't talk to her. He had completely shut down.

As we worked through the program, this boy eventually started talking to his mother again. At first she didn't like what he had to say, because he was expressing the anger and negative feelings he had been holding inside. But to her credit, she was happy that her son was finally speaking, and she continued to work with me and with him. As the weeks passed, their relationship healed.

The mother was so impressed with the results that she enrolled her other sons in the program too.

That was my first repeat business.

One boy came to the group with his father, who had been absent but returned to his son's life and wasn't happy with what he saw when he returned. He especially worried about his son's drug use. He told me, "I know my son smokes pot. I don't like it."

That father was convinced that I would never be able to get his son to admit that he smoked marijuana, let alone convince him to give it up. But as the boy worked through his wounds, by the end of the program he not only admitted that he smoked pot, but also pledged to stop the self-medicating behavior and use a punching bag when he got angry or hurt.

His father was so happy, and so moved, that he cried at the graduation.

The other five boys who participated in that first group also changed and grew dramatically. It was gratifying to me both to make it happen and to watch it happen, week after week. My extensive research and all the hands-on work I had done paid off to fulfill my vision. I could help boys heal.

The Quest Project® worked.

While I was happy with my results, I was also completely exhausted. It took ten years of ten-week sessions for me to realize that working so intensely with eight kids was too much. I cut the number of boys in each session to five, and I made other changes as I noticed where the boys were getting stuck and what additional help they needed to move forward.

One fundamental change was how I interacted with the parents. When I launched the program, I included two parent-only meetings focused on skill-building. At the beginning of the program we met to prepare the parents for the upcoming changes and teach them how to work with their boys in the weeks ahead. At the end of the program we met to help the families move forward and continue to progress after their boys graduated.

When I asked for feedback at the end of the program, parents said, "I wish there was more parent involvement," or, "I feel like I'm on the outside." They were asking to be more involved, which is exactly what I wanted to hear. Children do well when their parents care enough to spend time with them. I was happy to add more parent meetings to the schedule.

I have increased the number of parent-only sessions from two to five, so that parents not only get the support and learn the skills they need to work with their children, but they also receive guidance in their own process. Parents also experience pain during the program, because confronting past experiences brings up a lot of emotions for everyone concerned. At the same time, they need help adjusting to what their boys are experiencing.

The boys changed, and they changed quickly. By the third week, they were already so different that parents were asking, "What is going on with my son?" I realized I needed to get ahead of that, so now I prepare the parents from the beginning. I tell them, "If your son's a quiet kid, he's going to be a loud kid; if he's a loud kid, he's going to be a quiet kid. If he's a normal kid, he's going to be a bizarre kid. If you have a bizarre kid, he's going to be normal." At first, parents can be confused and even upset with these kinds of changes, but the end results are worth it.

After fifteen years, more than 1,500 boys have graduated from The Quest Project®, and they're all making their mark in the world in their own way. One works for the space program at NASA. One is an NHL hockey player. One boy who told me he wanted to be a serial killer is now a lawyer. One is a dentist.

Many are firemen. Every once in a while I'll hear that one of my graduates is going to be a counselor. One young man who completed the program plans to send his own son to The Quest Project®.

This makes me extremely proud.

What is it about The Quest Project® that sparks these dramatic transformations? In the next chapter, I'll share an overview of how The Quest Project® progresses, week by week. You will learn what issues I deal with and the way the program addresses them. You'll learn how I help boys heal their pain and move beyond the self-destructive behaviors that pain causes. Even if you cannot enroll your son in The Quest Project®, the next chapters will give you insight into how to help your son face and work through his own challenges.

Some of these activities come with a strong "Don't Try This at Home!" warning label. As a trained and licensed therapist I have experience with highly emotional people, and I know how to handle intense situations. Also, because I am an outsider, it is much easier for me to be objective than it is for the parents who love and worry about their sons.

To help you apply some of The Quest Project® techniques with your own child and get the most out of this book, I conclude each step in the program with special tips and modifications designed especially for mothers (and some fathers) who want to work with their boys on their own. These tips appear under the heading *What Mom Can Do*.

Here are some things to remember before we begin:

1. Before working with your child, it's important to be informed. Read as much as you can about adolescent boys and the challenges they face. Keep a journal of your own thoughts and get counseling to clarify

your intent and formulate a plan to organize, schedule, and work with your son.

2. Form a group with other mothers or parents for support and feedback as you go through the process. Your son might not need this, but chances are you will!

3. Set a schedule and get feedback from your son about your plans before you start. For best results, it's important (but not absolutely necessary) that he feel like a willing participant in whatever work you do. (Also, remember, this is tough love time, and what happens is ultimately up to you.)

4. Buy a punching bag (I'll explain later).

5. Ask your son's father or other healthy males in your community to help mentor your son through this process.

6. Keep it simple, especially when you discuss feelings with your son. I limit my discussions of feelings to what I call "The Big Four"—Mad, Sad, Glad, and Afraid.

7. Start each time with your son by offering a treat you know he likes— pizza and soda, ice cream, etc. The treat doesn't need to be food-related, but it should be something simple to set a positive mood before you get to work.

8. Outline any natural consequences that may be necessary to get the ball rolling.

Stay positive and expect some difficult times. Change doesn't happen overnight. If you find yourself or your son struggling with these exercises, get some professional help.

CHAPTER 6

The Quest Project®—An Overview

The Quest Project® lasts approximately ten weeks, during which time the boys attend ten group sessions, usually one per week, for ninety minutes. The project also includes five parent meetings: one at the beginning, one at the end, and three at crucial points in the middle of the program when parents need the most support.

I facilitate separate age-appropriate groups for boys ages 11-13, 14-16 and 17-19, so the boys who work together are in a similar place developmentally, can relate to each other as peers, and feel comfortable sharing their experiences. Each group is limited to five boys, so each boy receives the time and attention he needs.

Week 1 – Container Building

Remember how I said that every quest begins with a question? The Quest Project® is no different, and it starts with this one:

"How the HELL are you tonight?"

Chances are that question is not what you expected from a mental health professional. I apologize if it offends you, but at the same time, I want you to understand my reason for kicking off ten weeks of intensive, personal psychological work with a four-letter word.

I need the boys to trust me.

I want them to understand from that first moment that I'm not a parent or a teacher or a coach. I'm not on a pedestal looking down on them, and my purpose is not to judge, correct or shame them, or tell them how to be. I'm a mentor with special skills, and I use those skills for only one reason—to help them make their lives better.

After the expletives are out of the way, I devote the first meeting to what I call "Container Building." This is based on the premise that meaningful work needs a safe container. Our meeting place must be safe, where the boys can feel secure sharing deep, personal things they've probably never talked about with anyone before. We establish right away that what happens in our meetings is confidential. What is said here stays here. The boys can feel free to express themselves, four-letter words and all. The exception(s) to the confidentiality rule are for boys who demonstrate suicidal or homicidal ideation—basically, an intention to harm themselves or others—and for boys who have been abused or have perpetrated abuse. I am legally obligated to report those cases.

Once they know that it is safe to be honest about who they are, each boy introduces himself and tells his story about why he thinks he's in the program. Then he tells his story about why his parents say he's there.

(Those are usually two totally different stories.)

As the boys share their stories, something powerful happens. They start to realize they are not alone. "Oh, there's another guy with a story like mine." "I'm not so different." "I'm not a freak." This levels the playing field and creates a supportive community where work can be done and changes can be made.

What Mom Can Do:

The best-case scenario before you begin is to see a counselor for yourself for at least three visits to help you set things up. Setting things up means stating your intent and building your "container" with a conscious plan that you will keep in front of you on a schedule.

The first week, ask your son to write down what his "fantasy parent" would look like, and write down your own fantasy of what your perfect parent would have been when you were growing up. Then share them, without judging or over-talking. Tip: Short and sweet works best with boys.

Week 2 – Goal Setting

When I went on my Vision Quest, I retreated into the woods knowing I wanted to heal myself to become the man I wanted to be. I had that goal going in.

The boys who come to me are still kids, so most of them don't have clear goals, except maybe for Mom to get off their back. If you're going to get anywhere, you need to have a goal. So the second week's meeting is dedicated to Goal Setting. We get to this quickly, because it's important for the boys to know what they are working towards.

We set goals together, as a group, but we don't do it the way it's done in school. I do it in a way that resonates with boys, feels real to them, and helps them to visualize and feel connected to their future.

I use a visual and physical process that involves very specific guided imagery to help each boy discover the man he will become, or the man he wants to be. I help the boys identify and name the primary things that block them from that goal. This gives each boy a clear picture of what he will be working to overcome in the course of the program and beyond.

The point of Goal Setting is to establish a direction and a purpose for the boys and to give some meaning to their life. It helps them understand, "There's a better place than where I'm at right now, and I can get there, and this is where it starts." It also helps them understand what is blocking them from moving forward.

What Mom Can Do:

Practice this exercise at home on yourself. Visualize the woman you want to be and what might be standing in your way. Then ask your son to visualize the man he is going to become, as well as whatever is blocking him from getting there. Afterwards, share your visualizations, but remember, no judgments. You just want to help your son think in a different way about his life and the challenges he faces.

Week 3 – The Tool Box

Pain is almost always what's behind adolescent boys' problem behavior. Most boys, no matter how "normal" and healthy their upbringing, possess a wound of which they are not even conscious. That's just part of growing up.

In the third week, we address and deal with that pain in an exercise I call the "Tool Box." Inside this metaphorical box are the unconscious messages, both negative and positive, that the boys have received and internalized over the course of their lives. Since part of this exercise includes figuring out where those internalized messages come from, many boys will discover, "My mom and dad have given me a bunch of shit!"

I promise, there is a very good reason I put the boys (and their parents) through this discovery. As in therapy, we have to go through the crap to heal the crap. I help boys identify the crap. As it turns out, getting them to identify it is a side door into making them accountable for it. Plus, when they understand that they weren't born with this negative thing, that someone else actually put it there by judging them or criticizing them or otherwise sending them a negative message, they feel like they can then give that message back to the responsible party.

And yes, that responsible party is usually one or both of their parents. That's why one of the parent meetings is held before this session—to help the parents deal with the anger sparked by this exercise.

I don't send the boys home to their parents with only these negative feelings to process. After we uncover the crap, we finish off the exercise by retrieving the positive messages that they also might not be conscious they've received, including messages of being wanted and loved by their parents.

The session ends on this decidedly high note. Still, Week 3 is a tough week. It's a dive into the muck, it's the first week the boys go deep into their feelings, and it forces them to look at painful things that they have likely avoided dealing with. I encourage parents to be ready, because after this session many of the boys will act out. When they go through something this painful, boys tend to act out verbally and physically.

Hence, the reason to buy a punching bag before the program starts. Punching bags are the best outlet for boys to release their anger, because they are built for just one purpose—to take a punch! Boys are very tactile, meaning they need to feel the crunch in their hands and the strength and power of their muscles. This tells them they have released the uncomfortable feeling of anger.

What Mom Can Do:

If possible, walk through or get coaching on this exercise from your counselor first. Guide your son through a similar exercise, helping him uncover the negative messages he's storing inside. Help him identity positive messages, too. Do the exercise with him to let him know you're working together. Reveal some of the negative messages you might be carrying, as well as some of the positive ones, to give your son an idea of how the exercise works and to put yourself on a level playing field with him.

Week 4 – Clean Up

Week 4 is another difficult, emotional week. I call this week's exercise "Clean Up," because this is where we work to uncover the rest of each boy's pain by diving even deeper into his story and uncovering more wounds he might not know he's carrying. Once he has identified these wounds, he is finally ready to wipe the slate clean and begin to heal.

I use another visualization exercise to accomplish this. The exercise helps identify wounds, both physical and emotional, that they may not have received as messages, but that happened as a result of memorable events. We uncover them by having each boy draw on a map of his body where various injuries happened and what those events were. For example, I tell all the boys to start by drawing a broken heart, because that is typically why they initially came to counseling.

The events the boys reveal include things like falling off a skateboard or suffering through the chicken pox. They may also include abuse and extremely traumatic experiences, which is why this week can be painful and difficult. We dig down deep to uncover anything and everything negative that the boys might be holding onto. The idea is that once they see or hit bottom, they can start to build back up.

What Mom Can Do:

While it is fine to attempt your own version of the exercise I use in the program, I don't advise a non-professional to deal with serious issues like abuse. PTSD can be severe, and you need a professional to help guide your son through it. However, if you stick to smaller wounds, like breaking up with a girlfriend or feeling shamed in school or at home or low self-esteem, you can keep your son moving forward, while using what he reveals to de-termine if you might need the help of a professional.

Be willing to share some of your own wounds that you have worked through first. This gives your son permission to be human, and painting a picture for him is an effective form of mentoring.

Week 5 – The Anger Shadow

Anger is the messiest part of life. It makes people lose control. Anger drives people to say and do stupid, even dangerous, things. It's a major reason why a lot of boys come to The Quest Project® to begin with.

However, while a lot of people have anger problems, in Week 5 I stress to these boys that their anger isn't the problem. It's how the boys deal with their anger, how it makes them behave, that gets them into trouble. This week's exercise is called the "Anger Shadow."

To help the boys feel comfortable opening up about their anger, I spend some time talking about my own anger. I show them the hand I broke in a fight, and I talk about the messes I made in my life by not owning my anger, both as a teenager and as an adult. I explain how I eventually identified my own Anger Shadow (my term for what I did when I was angry), as well as what I did to change it. This gives the boys a sense of how the process works and how they might deal with their own anger.

After telling them my story, I talk with each boy about his anger and how it gets him in trouble. The boys typically say things like, "When I get angry, I punch holes in the wall," or, "When I get angry, I push my sister and brother around," or, "When I get angry, I smoke pot." Some of the boys turn their anger inward, cutting themselves or burning their skin with cigarettes.

Because different things happen in school than at home, I ask each boy to identify three things he does at home and three things he does at school (things like walking out of class, talking back to the teacher, slamming his locker, getting in fights). Then we get to the change part. I ask each boy to choose a new behavior that he will use the next time he feels angry. Here's where the punching bag comes into play.

Ultimately, each boy commits to a new, healthier way to deal with his anger, both at home and at school, and publicly states what he will do the next time he gets angry. The point of this exercise is to help the boys understand that it's okay to get angry, that anger is normal, and that they just need to learn better ways to express and deal with that anger. A message of "Don't be angry" is counter-productive. It says, "You're wrong for being angry," and thus he feels something is wrong with him. Self-esteem is then damaged and usually results in compartmentalizing the anger, causing responses like "My anger made me do it," or "It's my anger," instead of him owning the behavior.

What Mom Can Do:

We all get angry, so this one should be easy! Start by sharing some stories of your own anger and some of the things you've done that you maybe wish you hadn't. Some of these actions may have involved your son. When you own up to bad behavior that he remembers, you foster trust.

You can then talk about what you will do in the future to handle your own anger more constructively. And of course, encourage your son to share his own stories, as well as his own ideas for new ways to deal with his anger—including using the punching bag!

Week 6 – Anger Work

In Week 6 all our work with anger begins to pay off. This is an initiation week, and now the boys deal with their anger in a powerful, meaningful way. I call this week's exercise "Anger Work," and boys often call it a highlight of The Quest Project®.

The power revolves around our evening ritual, a ritual designed to release anger in the most cathartic and complete way possible. The atmosphere is reminiscent of Native American initiation ceremonies, complete with incense and drums. Before we begin, I tell the boys that this night will change their lives forever, that this is when they shed their boy skin, and the man emerges.

I start by asking each boy, one by one, to visualize and identify his anger. Once this happens, they access their anger and bring it to the surface.

Then, they each let loose on the punching bag. I let them hit the bag with a baseball bat—not something I advocate doing at home. However, in this controlled environment the process is extremely emotional and cathartic. In a typical group of five, some boys will continue to hit the bag for ten to twenty minutes straight. I've seen boys throw up, and I've seen one nearly pass out. One or two are usually fighting back tears by the end, because behind the anger is sadness.

When the boys are done, they stand up. I tell them that they are no longer little boys, they are now young men. And with that comes responsibility.

In this ritual they have released so much anger, and the next step is for them to take in what they want. They get to choose what goes into the void, and with a hint from me, they choose joy. Whatever joy is for each boy, he identifies it. And since he is now a young man, he accepts responsibility for providing it.

After this session the boys typically go home bright-eyed and worn out, but also vulnerable, because this exercise lifts the lid off of their depression.

What Mom Can Do:

If you haven't already, now is the time to pull out that punching bag. Maybe even take turns whacking it, talking about what makes you angry and getting your anger out. Just please remember, fists are fine. I don't recommend using the bat without supervision, especially with the younger boys (aged eleven to thirteen).

Week 7 – Conflict Resolution

When the boys come for our seventh meeting, the change in them is visible. They walk tall. They look proud. There is a connection between them as individuals, because they have revealed their true selves to each other and grown through the experience. From now on, they are a circle of young men.

As young men they are expected to take responsibility for the issues that upset them and work toward resolving them. This week introduces a technique for conflict resolution. Each boy starts by identifying a conflict with a parent. Then we use the tool to work through a specific conflict resolution that allows both sides to be heard and a deeper understanding to be reached.

Just because a boy expresses what he wants doesn't mean he's going to get it. This process is primarily about understanding that there are two sides to the conflict, and that it can be discussed calmly. I teach the parents to use the same tool, which walks both participants through each of several steps while the other listens. The listener then repeats back what the other person says, to ensure that they heard it correctly.

When the exercise is finished, each person better knows and understands how the other person feels. Understanding goes a long way toward resolving conflict.

The exercise is designed for the boys and their parents to work on at home. During the session we do another exercise in our space that I call Dad/Not Dad. It dramatizes the difficult choice most boys believe they are facing: "Will I grow up to be like my dad, or NOT like my dad?" Boys with Absent Fathers have an especially hard time making this choice, between *emulating* a person who has hurt and disappointed them and trying to *eliminate* any trace of their father in their personality.

Through a visualization exercise the boys learn that there is a third way. They learn that instead of having to choose between being "like Dad" or "not like Dad," they can choose to be true to themselves. This allows them to be like their father in the ways that they admire without feeling destined or doomed to be like him in every way. They learn that they are not their father—they are their father's son.

For a lot of the boys, this is the first time they realize that they have a choice and that it's not a black-and-white choice to be or not to be their father. Learning that they can be exactly who they want to be is empowering.

What Mom Can Do:

I assign the conflict resolution exercise to the parents of the boys in my program, so it's something you can easily do with your son at home. Go to ClaytonLessor.com to download the worksheet.

If possible, enlist a mediator, especially the first time you try the exercise, to keep you on task and to help make the experience more enjoyable.

Moms should not attempt to facilitate the Dad/Not Dad exercise, as this can be a highly emotionally charged process. Instead, I recommend a male mentor or mental health professional who can work through this with your son.

Week 8 – The Gift

Week 8's exercise is based on the fairy tale *Iron Hans,* in which a boy loses his "Gift" (a golden ball), and later embarks on a hero's journey to find it. The boys in my program are guided through a visualization in which they lose their Gift because their parents haven't acknowledged it and made it feel real, something parents tend to do unconsciously. The boys are encouraged to feel anger and sadness at the loss, which is appropriate grief work.

The rest of the visualization takes the boys through each step of the hero's journey, a quest to recover the Gift. Growth happens at each stage of the journey, and when the exercise is finished, each boy recognizes that his Gift is a part of himself—the quality that he considers special and powerful. The boys name their Gifts. I hear, "My gift is my athletic ability," or, "My gift is my mechanical inclination," or, "My gift is my sense of humor," or simply, "My gift is my ability to be good."

This exercise gives each boy an opportunity to publicly identify his true strength, as opposed to what he has been told he's good at. There's a big difference between the two, and this is each boy's chance to express and claim what he knows in his heart makes him special. It teaches them to articulate not only that they are unique and talented, but exactly how and why. That makes it real.

What Mom Can Do:
This exercise works best as a sharing exercise, meaning you get to participate too. Encourage your son to open up and talk about the gifts he knows he has by first knowing and sharing your own and how you use them in the world. When it's your son's turn, remember not to question, judge, or suggest what you think his gifts are. Give him the freedom to express what he knows is true about himself, as opposed to what other people might have told him about himself.

Week 9 – Relationships and Forgiveness

Boys who have Absent Fathers often grow up lacking crucial information about Relationships, from how to have a healthy one with a partner to the basic birds-and-bees information. My hope is for your son to enjoy healthy, meaningful Relationships as he grows older, so Relationships are the theme for Week 9. We spend time talking about what love means, the difference between "love" and "in love," and even a little bit about sex (as is age-appropriate for the group).

We move to the topic of Forgiveness, because Forgiveness is essential to a healthy Relationship. Now that they've done their anger work, they're shown how to use the same conflict resolution process we introduced last week. We ask, "Who do I need to forgive in my life?"

They've all got somebody!

Most of the boys are trying to forgive a specific person, usually a parent. However, what most boys don't realize going into the exercise is that the primary person they need to forgive is themselves. In this exercise they talk through the process to reach that moment of Forgiveness.

What Mom Can Do:

Read, learn, and define what "love" and "in love" mean to you. Read and learn as much as you can about the topic of Forgiveness, as it is important to process this for yourself before you can help your son. You can then work through the conflict resolution exercise from last week with a new focus on Forgiveness. Start with someone you need to forgive and model the process for your son. Then give him a turn to forgive someone.

Week 10 – Purpose = Mission

Until they come to me, the boys I work with (and nearly all boys) are bombarded with "don't be" messages. "Don't be like your father." "Don't be stupid." "Don't be lazy." "Don't be bad." Those messages come from parents, from teachers, and from society as a whole. They are not intended to do any harm, but in my expert opinion, they don't help.

"Don't be" messages don't give a boy direction toward what he wants to be, only what he's not supposed to be.

At our final meeting before graduation, I have the boys focus on what they want to be. I ask them to choose concrete actions to make it happen. I call the exercise "Purpose = Mission," and it's designed to designate their path as young men. It's a vision to work toward and a way to use their newfound skills. The boys can then take what they've learned in the program into the world, make a difference, and make a good life for themselves. As an example, I tell the boys my mission is: "To create healthy lifestyles by teaching, facilitating, and example."

> *What Mom Can Do:*
> *Start with baby steps, like formulating your own mission statement and sharing it with your son. Then help your son share his vision of what he wants to accomplish. Work with him to develop an action plan to succeed. Remember, this is about what he wants, not what you want, and your job is to support the vision for his future that excites him.*

Graduation

A number of cultural initiation rituals end with a celebration, with food and a ceremony, to mark the fact that the boy is now a man. The Quest Project® concludes with a serious, emotional graduation ceremony. Each boy stands before his parents, his peers, and the entire group to say, "This is who I am now."

At the ceremony I give each boy a gift to signify what he has achieved. At the end of a Vision Quest in a native culture, a boy who has gone into the wilderness might come back with an animal pelt or a tiger tooth—an ornament to mark the passage. I present each boy with a talisman that represents the work he has done and the wound he has healed, so he will never forget what he accomplished in The Quest Project®.

I also encourage the parents to give their son a verbal gift, to let him know that they recognize his accomplishment, that he has changed and is no longer a little boy.

The ceremony is an emotional and meaningful conclusion for the program. It holds space for the boys to celebrate their success and reconnect with their parent or parents as the young men they have become.

What Mom Can Do:

Celebrate your son's accomplishment with a small gift, a special meal, and verbal recognition of his success. Remember, this is hard work for a young, vulnerable person who is still somewhat irrational and not fully developed. Even if you have seen only small, minimal steps, the seeds have been planted and will germinate at his pace. Celebrate!

I developed The Quest Project® over many years through a combination of intensive research and personal experience. Part of the reason it works so well is that parents are not present. The boys have a safe place to say things that might hurt their parents or make them angry. Therefore, you can't replicate at home what I do in my office. Still, I have shared each step of the program to illustrate that in the path toward healing, each point in the progression builds on the one before. Understanding the steps of The Quest Project® may give you ideas to help your son progress through his own transition to manhood.

The most important gift you can give your child is the one you are giving him right now, reading this book. It shows that you care, that you're interested, and that you want to be the best parent you can be. I encourage you to try some of the solutions, suggestions, and exercises presented here. You don't need to be perfect. You just need to be there.

My goal is to take The Quest Project® into more communities so I can help boys everywhere benefit from the structure of the program and the experience of sharing it with a community of their peers. If you'd like to learn more about the program or how I might work with your son, contact me through ClaytonLessor.com.

CHAPTER 7

Case Studies

In my history of running The Quest Project®, I've worked with all kinds of adolescent boys, representing a wide range of races, socioeconomic backgrounds, and even sexual orientations. Some were referred to me through their schools, some through other therapists, and many were referred by parents of boys who had participated in the program and were happy with the results.

Regardless of their differences, in my experience the overwhelming majority of the boys who have completed The Quest Project® have followed a similar trajectory: They've confronted their anger, healed their pain, found purpose and direction in their lives, and ultimately have grown and changed for the better. They have transformed from troubled boys into fine young men, and each of them makes me proud of their work and the role I've been able to play in their lives.

It is my privilege to introduce you to a few of them now.

Eight boys and their families have volunteered to share their stories in this book, speaking openly about what brought them to me, what their experience in The Quest Project® was like, and how that experience changed them and prepared them for the future.

My hope is that by meeting these boys and their families and reading their stories, you might recognize similar issues or problems that you experience with your son. By learning how these boys confronted their issues and moved beyond them, you'll see that healing and growth are possible for your son as well.

All names and certain specific details have been changed in the interest of protecting the privacy of these boys and their families. Beyond that, all of these stories are true. I hope you will find them as inspirational as I do.

CHAPTER 8

Dylan

I f it seems that your adolescent son gets angrier as he gets older, it's probably not your imagination. The hormones associated with puberty can transform even the calmest child into a teenage version of The Incredible Hulk. That may be why anger is one of the most common problems I deal with in my practice and in The Quest Project®.

I'm not saying anger is a bad thing. As I mentioned earlier, anger is a normal part of life. We all experience it, including me. The problem isn't the anger itself, but how we express and deal with anger. Since most of us aren't born knowing how to handle anger, that means we have to learn to deal with it as it arises in our lives.

Take the case of Dylan.

Dylan is the youngest of three children, although he is a twin who was delivered by Cesarean section, so his position in the birth order was kind of luck of the draw. According to his mom, as you might expect with twin boys, he and his brother were more than a handful from birth.

Dylan's Mother: *They're both incredibly energetic and always have been. When they were little, I would open the front door and have them run around the house—because we didn't have a fenced yard—and just keep running around the house. Because they always had so much energy. They were exhausting. It was like that from the minute they woke up* *until the minute they went to bed. And literally, you would put them in bed, turn around, and they would be asleep.*

Like a lot of brothers, especially brothers who are close in age, Dylan and his twin didn't always get along.

Dylan's Mother: *They both would be somewhat aggressive when they didn't get their way. They fought a lot. I remember them, three or four years old, and literally one had the other under his arm, yelling. Sometimes, honestly, it's hard for me to remember who did what between the two of them.*

Looking for a way to channel some of their boys' boundless energy, Dylan's parents involved the twins in sports as soon as they were old enough to play. Both boys excelled, and Dylan became one of his school's top athletes. However, his success in athletics did not calm his temper.

Dylan's Father: *There's been a long-standing tendency for him to be angry when he gets emotional. He's reactive, angry and reactive.*

Dylan's father witnessed his son's anger most in practice and in competition. The pressure to perform, combined with his explosive temper, meant a mistake would often lead to an emotional, violent, and sometimes public outburst.

Dylan's Father: *I was often the last one coming out of the locker-room with a very emotional kid. He's got pretty good abilities. But if it doesn't go right, oof!*

Dylan's mother found Dylan's anger more troubling. It became more of a problem after she and Dylan's father separated. Dylan was thirteen, just entering adolescence, a point when even a less emotional boy might start to experience more anger. For Dylan, it was a perfect storm.

Dylan's Father: *They (Dylan and his siblings) were very shocked by it—we weren't a marriage where we were fighting or screaming. And so it did make it hard for him. He seemed to get angrier, violent. There was suddenly an emotional change. He got more verbally abusive to his siblings and to his mom. He started talking very negatively to her.*

Dylan's Mother: *It was a huge catalyst. Before the divorce he would get angry and aggressive with me, but it really escalated once we were separated. And I didn't have anybody there to back me up.*

Dylan never harmed his mother physically during his rages. But as things continued to escalate, she worried that without his father to stop him, he might turn his anger on her—especially after she saw what he had done to his bedroom.

Dylan's Father: *The door to his bedroom is torn off, the door to his bathroom in his room torn off, the hole in the wall, the lamp, just violence...*

Dylan's Mother: *He would take a bat to the wall of his bedroom and just beat huge holes in it. The dry wall in there is trashed from his anger. Those were the episodes that scared me the most.*

Dylan didn't mean to upset or frighten his mother. When an adolescent boy gets angry and acts out, inside he's still a little boy, crying out to be understood. Unfortunately, when that little boy is suddenly the size and strength of a man, he can do extensive damage.

Dylan had real, valid reasons to be angry beyond hormonal changes, and even beyond the pressures of being a young athlete. His parents' divorce ripped his world apart. Just a year before, his family had moved into their dream home, a house his parents redesigned from top to bottom to be a haven for their kids and their friends.

> **Dylan's Mother:** *They had their own rooms, they did their own things, they had all these friends around them—there were a ton of kids in the neighborhood. It was a great place.*

After only one year, Dylan had to leave this dream home and move into a new, smaller place, leaving his father and his friends behind.

> **Dylan's Mother:** *I moved into a condo, my ex moved into an apartment. The boys are back to sharing a room, they are not close to their friends—they've had a shit couple of years.*

As hard as he tried, Dylan could not make sense of what had happened to his life and his world. Why did his parents split up if it was just making everyone miserable?

> **Dylan's Mother:** *He repeatedly asked, "Was this really a mutual decision?" Because that's what we told him. He was looking for someone to blame because he was still really wounded about it.*

Research shows that with most boys, anger is also a symptom of depression. Below the anger that they show to the world is the hidden sadness and fear that drives the anger and rage. That was what Dylan went through. If your son seems angry a lot of the time, chances are good he's hiding some sadness and fear too.

> **Dylan:** *I remember crying a lot, because I was upset too. And then one day I was angry—and I would throw stuff and put holes in the walls.*

Dylan's mother knew that her son (and her walls) needed help. She and Dylan's father were both worried about their son. If what he was feeling inside was as extreme and dramatic as what he showed to the outside world, they were afraid he might turn to drugs or alcohol to self-medicate and make the pain go away.

Dylan's Mother: *He would be so intense and so focused that you'd just look at him and know he'd have to do something for release. And if we didn't figure out how to get something, he was going to find it somewhere. Nobody can keep going like that. At some point, you have to have the release, and it's not going to matter where it comes from.*

Dylan's Father: *I didn't want to lose him mentally, emotionally, have him be gone. I didn't have a sense he had done anything like that, but I wasn't sure. I struggled with drugs and alcohol as a kid. I didn't want him to start heading down the path I did. That was my fear.*

Dylan's parents sought a therapist for Dylan to talk to, hoping this might help him feel better and keep his problems from further escalating. Unfortunately, it did not. Dylan didn't feel like he was being helped.

Dylan: *It felt weird. We never actually talked about my anger. We never really focused on it, and it was just kind of awkward. He was really into technology—electronics—so we talked about that for a while. I almost fell asleep a few times. It was weird to say the least.*

Dylan found himself at the same place so many of the boys I see with anger issues wind up—in a psychiatrist's office getting a prescription to medicate for ADHD. Being in a new environment and constantly shuttling back and forth between his parents' homes made it hard for Dylan to get into a routine. He wasn't consistent about taking his meds, and nothing changed. The rages continued, as did the damage to his walls.

Dylan: *I didn't have a way of calming myself down.*

Dylan's Mother: *Next to him going and using (drugs or alcohol) and doing something totally destructive, I don't know that it could have gotten a whole lot worse.*

Dylan's mother understood that her son was hurting. She understood that he needed help. But she had no idea what to do that could possibly make a difference.

Dylan's Mother: *How do you teach that it's okay to have emotions but not do damage? How do I teach him that it's really okay to have these feelings—I get that you're pissed, I'm pissed too! But how do you teach that? That was really the piece I knew he needed help with. He's got these feelings, he's got all this stuff going on, and he needs to have them, but they need to be able to come out in a safe way.*

Then his parents discovered The Quest Project®.

Dylan's Mother: *I was looking for any avenue. I didn't know what it was going to look like. We needed to do something, and so I was asking around and talking to people and finding out stuff. It happened to be somebody that my ex-husband knew; a friend of his had a son who had gone through the program.*

Dylan's father found out about me, and he and Dylan's mother decided to bring him in to talk to me. For Dylan, this didn't feel like particularly good news.

Dylan's Mother: *He wasn't happy about it. He didn't want to have to go see yet another therapist. But he also knew he was in enough trouble—he was having problems with grades, we set some boundaries with sports, and he wasn't living up to that end of the bargain. He knew the interventions wouldn't end until something worked.*

Dylan's father was the one who finally brought Dylan to meet me.

Dylan's Father: *He didn't want to go, he thought it would be a waste of time, we tried this stuff before, yada, yada, yada. But I was prepared to do whatever it took to get him there.*

Before I met with Dylan, I sat down with each of his parents individually to get their take on the situation. Then I met with Dylan alone. We all decided that he was a great candidate for The Quest Project®. Well, all of us except Dylan.

Dylan: *I definitely did not want to go. I never had been in a group before, I didn't know what the other kids would think, so I was really nervous.*

However, Dylan didn't have a choice in the matter. He was enrolled in the program, and soon it was his turn to stand up in front of a room full of strange boys and talk about his problems.

Dylan: *It was a little nerve wracking. I was the first person to talk about this, about what I was doing and stuff like that, and I didn't know if I was going to be the most severe and kids were going to be scared of me or think I was weird.*

One thing worked in Dylan's favor from the beginning. He wanted to change, and he was open to it. He learned quickly that having the support of other boys his age—other boys who also had problems—wasn't scary at all. The group might even help him accomplish his goal.

Dylan: *It turns out my problem wasn't as bad as I thought it was. The kids were shaking their heads, going along with it, understanding that I knew I wanted to work on it.*

Dylan's father picked him up after the first meeting and immediately noticed a difference in his son.

Dylan's Father: *He looked tired. I know he didn't dig into anything deep, but he had this air of surrender, I guess. I didn't push too much, and he didn't want to tell me too much. He just said it was cool, he liked Clayton.*

By the time the next Monday rolls around, he goes, "Hey, do I have Clayton tonight?"

From then on, getting Dylan to group was never an issue.

Dylan's Mother: *It was always a positive thing.*

Dylan: *The kids were nice and funny, and Clayton was nice too, and we always had pizza, and the food was always good, and it was something different every time. I liked it a lot. Eventually I was excited and couldn't wait to go.*

One big reason why I believe the meetings work as well as they do is that what happens inside our meetings is confidential. The boys know they can say anything they want or need to say, because at the very first meeting we all promise each other that what happens in group stays in group. Every boy can feel safe sharing what he's experiencing and processing his feelings. He can work on what he wants to work on.

I also advise parents not to ask too many questions about what the boys experience during our meetings. Part of what they need—and part of what Dylan needed—is time to process their feelings and work through them on their own, without their parents intruding, judging, or even trying to help.

Dylan's Mother: *I really tried to stay out of it and let that process take care of itself. Sometimes I would just ask him, "Hey, how was it?" or, "How are you?" If he wanted to talk about it, great, but if he didn't, I just let it go. I figured that was his sacred place, not mine to get involved in.*

A lot of what Dylan did in this safe space was healing the wounds behind his anger. Through the weekly exercises he was encouraged to think about and confront the source of his pain, instead of continuing to mask it and hide it like he did in his normal life. This process is necessary, but it also brings that pain to the surface, which makes it much more tangible in a boy's life. Most boys will react to this. That's why I tell parents to expect things to get worse before they get better.

> **Dylan's Father:** *He had seething anger at me. Before it was more underlying. Now he was attacking me, calling me names, that kind of stuff. I tried to let it be, because I talked to Clayton. I understood that he was harboring resentment at me and I knew I made mistakes as a father. I let him have his anger, it's his right. That meant biting my tongue, turning my head, but still setting boundaries in subtle ways.*

Discovering the source of his pain wasn't easy for Dylan either, especially when I asked him to directly confront his anger in front of all the other boys during the Anger Song activity. Regardless of what kinds of things he said to his father, anger was the issue Dylan came to The Quest Project® to deal with, and in his mind dealing with it meant making it go away. So when he was encouraged to express it, he worried it might get out of control.

> **Dylan:** *I was scared. I was nervous and frightened at first. But once I understood the meaning of it, it definitely helped.*

Having the support of his peers and watching them confront their own anger made a big difference.

> **Dylan:** *I started to get into it and start demolishing the punching bag. Once I was done with it, it definitely felt good.*

As the weeks passed, Dylan's mother noticed that her boy was different.

Dylan's Mother: *The anger had calmed down, the aggression calmed down, he would be able to verbalize he needed space. We still had some ups and downs. He had worked to the point where he got his grades up, so we allowed him to play golf, and when his grades fell, we had no choice but to say, "You are off the golf team." That's hard when you're the star player. But the hitting things slowed down. It definitely decreased.*

Dylan's Father: *I started to notice when he would get angry, on his own he would try to find a way to express his anger. On the golf course, he'd go on the side, express his anger in a more appropriate way, rather than smashing his club into a tee box or on a green. Then he would come back and apologize, and he started to express how he felt. That was a real noticeable change. It's one of the first things I noticed about him, was an ability to talk through what's going on.*

And while Dylan figured out how to control his anger, his parents also learned a few things.

Dylan's Father: *Now, with some help from Clayton, we are going through some conflict resolution, him and me. We do that each week.*

Dylan's Mother: *One of the biggest things I learned was not to engage in any way. Dylan would be like, "Give me a reason, give me a reason, tell me why I can't," and then I'd tell him why and he'd say, "That's stupid." Whatever it was, he picked a fight. Being able to have that boundary of not engaging really helped me.*

I also learned that just because I experienced things that I thought were similar when I was a kid, like my parents getting divorced, doesn't mean that's how Dylan feels when he experiences it. That was really important to me to know as well. Just because I could maybe think I identify, really, unless I ask, I don't know.

Today, as I write this, Dylan has graduated from The Quest Project®. He's no longer taking ADHD medication. And he continues to improve.

Dylan's Father: *Clayton recommended along with working with his doctor that we stop the medication because he was so up and down with it. So we stopped and it became a non-factor.*

Dylan's Mother: *We've had a very pleasant summer. He's seeing Clayton one-on-one with his Dad, because I think there are some issues there that they are trying to work out. He's much more pleasant. He can still be verbally abusive, but I have set boundaries, and he is able to understand them.*

Before, that would have never happened. He would have been upset, belligerent, he would have been beating his wall with a baseball bat.

I asked Dylan why he thought The Quest Project® worked for him when nothing else did.

Dylan: *We did a lot of stuff to work through what we were going through versus just talking about it, and that made a big difference.*

For Dylan, finding a group of boys who were just like him, and learning how to face their issues and grow into manhood together, made the difference.

Dylan: *With Clayton and other kids I was in the group with, I always had a good feeling coming out of there. I knew I was trying to work on trying to fix me and my anger and stuff like that, but that made me have a good feeling walking out of there, it was always a good time really. We* *always had fun, found ways to joke around, and also at the same time accomplished stuff to help us out.*

Today, as he moves forward, his future looks bright.

Dylan: *I have better ways to handle my anger now, moving forward. I'm going to focus a lot more on my grades and try to get those a lot better, because that's going to be the most important thing for me next year before I do sports, really try to focus on my grades, get those up, and as long as I keep them up, focus a lot on sports and try and do the best I can.*

Dylan's Father: *I feel like he's got a much better chance of being the kid he can be.*

I feel that way too.

Andrew

In this work I deal with boys who act out, boys who get in trouble, boys who do the kinds of things that get them in hot water with their families, their schools. and even their communities. But boys who are in trouble aren't the only boys I see. I also see boys who are hurting who don't break the rules or hurt anyone else. Boys who are suffering in silence and who desperately need that suffering to end.

Andrew was one of those boys.

Andrew was bullied. From the time he was ten or eleven he was the kid other kids picked on. There was no glaringly obvious reason for this. He didn't have an extra nose or a funny voice or anything that would necessarily make him the target.

> **Andrew's Mother:** *I couldn't figure this whole thing out, because it's not like I had the kid going to school who dressed weird. To this day, I don't know why they chose him.*

Still, he was the one the bullies chose. Once he became that target, the target label stuck for years. He reached the point where he just couldn't take it anymore.

> **Andrew's Mother:** *I got up in the middle of the night to use the restroom, and I could hear a noise so I followed it. When I got to the noise, it was Andrew in his room. He was sitting on his bedroom floor— and it was like two in the morning—and he was just crying.*

I remember looking at him and saying, "Andrew, what's the matter?" He looked up at me and said, "Mom, I'm so sad inside. I don't even think it's worth it anymore."

He was about fourteen.

That's when Andrew's mother knew that her son had a problem and that she needed to do something to help him.

But what?

Unlike a lot of the kids I work with, Andrew grew up in an intact family. His mother and father parented him together. He never acted out or caused any trouble. His mother describes him as an ideal child who listened to his parents and did what he was told to do. He had friends and was happy, and his life seemed normal.

But once he hit the fourth grade, everything changed.

Andrew's Mother: I don't know what happened, exactly; kids started picking on him and he wouldn't defend himself. I raised him to turn the other cheek and walk away, to the point where he didn't defend himself.

It just escalated and got worse, up into high school. They didn't physically pick on him. It was just constant emotional abuse. And then other kids chimed in, and he couldn't make any friends.

Being bullied made doing the normal things children need to do to get through life almost too painful for Andrew to bear.

Andrew: I didn't want to go to school. I knew that they were going to pick on me and berate me every day. It would happen most days and put me into a depression, and it made focusing hard. I became reclusive, I didn't talk to people much. I would always look down at my feet and wouldn't make eye contact. I would hunch my shoulders over, looking at the ground.

For a mother who loves her son, watching your child suffer the pain of being bullied and being unable to help him is heartbreaking. Andrew's mom tried everything she could think of to stop the bullying. She started with the typical actions most mothers take when their child is being picked on. She tried to convince him the hurtful words didn't matter. She talked with Andrew about communication and about standing his ground. She tried to help him find the right words to stop the bullies. But they wouldn't stop.

Andrew's mother turned to the school for help to deal with the kids who made her son miserable. After all, it's the school's responsibility to make sure kids are safe there. At least Andrew's mother thought so.

Andrew's Mother: *I had a lot of meetings between teachers and super-intendents and counselors, and it just didn't do any good.*

The school never did anything, at least not anything that worked. Years went by and nothing changed. So Andrew's mother tried taking Andrew to counseling.

Andrew's Mother: *He didn't have any friends, he seemed sad, and I just thought that maybe it would help him. But basically they just gave him medicine for anxiety—which, who the heck wouldn't have anxiety? But they didn't do what I would call counseling. They did "Here's some medicine. How are you feeling this month?" More like psychiatry.*

Still, Andrew took the medication. If something might help him, if something might make his day-to-day life less painful, he and his mother were willing to try it. When your child is suffering like that, chances are you will do anything.

But nothing helped. And it certainly didn't stop the bullying. No pill can do that.

Andrew's Mother: *He was still walking into the same environment.*

The situation continued from elementary school through junior high. But after the night she found Andrew crying on his bedroom floor, Andrew's mother knew she couldn't let him suffer anymore. Her child, whom she loved, had told her that life was no longer worth living. She knew she had to get serious.

Andrew's Mother: *At that point he was in middle school, and he had said, "I just can't go." I had him sit at the table and write "first hour, second hour, third hour" on a piece of paper with the kids' names who were bothering him in those classes and what they were actually saying or doing.*

When he was done and handed me the paper, I realized a lot of it was the same kids in the same classes, almost every single day. So I told him we were going to have a meeting with the principal.

They met. Promises were made. Yet, again, nothing happened. Every time Andrew's mother asked for help with what her son was going through, she was not taken seriously. She was turned away. Nothing changed.

Well, that's not entirely true. Andrew changed. The stress of living with constant bullying developed into a case of Obsessive Compulsive Disorder, or OCD.

Andrew's Mother: *He would wash his hands constantly, and one time we were going to go somewhere, and he wouldn't touch anything. We were getting ready to leave, and he was taking his arm and trying to turn a door knob. I looked at him and said, "What are you doing? We have to go." He goes, "Well, I'm trying to get the door open." I'm like, "Just turn it," and he's like "No!" He would not touch that door knob.*

It got to the point where he was washing his hands so much that I had to pack his hands in Vaseline because they were so raw.

No matter what Andrew's mother did, nothing made things better. In fact, her kindhearted, gentle child—a boy who would never hurt anyone or anything— seemed to have a harder time with each passing year.

Eventually, Andrew made it to high school. But while the kids were getting older, they hadn't outgrown their need to bully him. Desperate, his mother went to the school again, almost demanding that they find some way to help her son.

They referred Andrew to a program that was a little unusual for a boy with his particular issues.

> **Andrew's Mother:** *I had gone to the school and asked them about counseling. They referred me to a place you could go to the hospital and stay there. I decided to check it out first, because the school had dropped the ball so much, so I wasn't going to take their word.*
>
> *I went up there and the lady started telling me about how the program worked. She said Andrew would stay there and I would bring his home-work, and they would get in groups and do discussions. I said, "What are the other kids like that are here?" She said, "Yours is unusual because most of them are addicted to drugs." I looked at her and said, "What we have here is a kid who doesn't have any friends and desperately wants a friend, and you want me to put him with kids who are addicted to drugs so he can get a drug addict for a friend?"*

Clearly, an inpatient residential program was not what Andrew needed. Luckily, the woman at the program realized this, and unlike the administrators at Andrew's school, she actually listened to Andrew's mother.

She gave Andrew's mother my card, and that's how I came to meet Andrew.

My first impression of Andrew was that he was incredibly polite. He was shy and slow to engage, but he felt safe with me, so we were able to work together.

First, we tackled the OCD, which we made short order of in just a few meetings. Since he had so many issues dealing with other boys, we met one-on-one for a while. Sometimes we would meet with his mother. Gradually we built trust.

I knew that The Quest Project®, being a weekly opportunity for him to interact with other boys, would be ideal for Andrew. Once he was stabilized, I told Andrew and his mother about the program and suggested he sign up for the next session. Andrew wasn't overly excited about the idea, but he agreed to go.

> **Andrew's Mother:** *I think he just thought, "I'm doing another counseling program, okay, whatever." At that point, he had pretty much given up.*

> **Andrew:** *I didn't know what to think. I figured it would either work or it wouldn't. Either way, I needed to do this to see what would happen. I figured it was worth the try.*

I was determined to make the program worth his effort. I wanted to help Andrew get past the pain of his everyday life so he could finish school, grow up, and become whatever he wanted to be without other people stopping him. Right away, the experience of being with the other boys—realizing that he could have relationships with them, that they would treat him with respect and even like him—made a difference.

But it wasn't easy at first.

> **Andrew:** *I think opening up was probably the hardest thing. You're talking to complete strangers, and it's hard to tell your personal business to your family sometimes—but somebody you only see once a week, it's really difficult and it's uncomfortable. That's your personal business; you don't really want to broadcast that. Especially since it hurts.*

The realization that he was not alone and that he was not the only boy with problems helped him to find his voice.

Andrew: *I don't remember the exact details of everyone's problems, but I do know that we were all there for our own specific reasons, and they were all personal and kind of harmful details, psychologically. We realized that these were things we needed to take care of, but it was harmful to us. We were upset about these problems.*

Dealing with those types of problems, even in a therapeutic setting, isn't easy. It's hard, sometimes painful work, for the boys and also for their parents.

Andrew's Mother: *At first it was okay, because it was mainly just, "How are things going at home?" and stuff like that. But Clayton did tell me in the first meeting, "Things are going to get worse before it gets better." And I guess I didn't believe him.*

He told me that was because instead of running to his safe haven—which was at home—Andrew was going to have to start dealing with these things and facing these things. He'd make him do these little homework assignments like writing down his feelings and would literally make him do things to face this.

And then he started getting angry. I had this kid that was very mild, and all of a sudden he's mad. It was just a switch and I wasn't used to it.

Most of the mothers I work with are like Andrew's mom. They are involved in their boys' lives and want the best for them and would do just about anything to help them. Because they are so concerned and so involved, some of them have issues with certain parts of the program. Seeing someone else (me) take over and put their sons through experiences that bring up painful feelings and difficult emotions is hard. It's hard to feel like a good mother if you're letting your son experience pain.

But this pain was necessary. Everything Andrew experienced in the program was monitored and guided, because he needed to find a way to get control of the situation. He needed to get to a point where whatever the bullies were saying to him and about him didn't matter. He needed to reach a place in his own heart and soul where their words no longer hurt him. Because there was nothing that he or I or anyone could do to change the bullies themselves. They were dealing with their own issues and needed their own kind of help.

The only solution to bullying, at least for a victim, is to work on yourself. That is what I helped Andrew accomplish, and it was extremely painful for his mother to watch. Even though the pain was necessary and would ultimately help him, Andrew's mother desperately wanted to make that pain go away. She instinctively wanted to step in and protect her child.

That meant I had to step in and stop her. More than once.

> *Andrew's Mother: I remember saying to Clayton, "You make me feel like I'm a bad mom, every time I come in here." He said, "I really think you're a good mom, but you've got to let him go through this. It's not anything you're doing. You just have to let him go through this."*
>
> *It took me a little bit to realize that talking with my son wasn't going to do it. They have to go through it and figure out how they can handle these things, what they can do to make their lives better. I guess he was just so angry inside, and I didn't really blame him. He just spent years going through this, and it was still going on.*

For Andrew, getting in touch with his anger was painful and frightening. But it was easier knowing that he wasn't doing it alone.

Andrew: *I wasn't really angry, but I did have a little anger built up. He had a punching bag, and we would hit it with a baseball bat. And I went crazy on it. When I came out afterwards, my mom and dad were wondering, "What did they do? Murder someone?" It was pretty bad. All the parents gave us all these weird looks because they heard us screaming and banging on the bags. They were probably thinking we were all nut jobs!*

I really did like that punching bag. It was a way to let loose like I've never done before. I was really quiet and reserved, so to let loose like that and let all my frustrations out was really fun. To see the other kids do it, see what they went through, was very inspiring—I'm not the only one who's going through this.

As the weeks went by, Andrew started to feel different about himself.

Andrew: *I developed a better sense of self-esteem. I realized that I need to think more of myself. I had a very low opinion of myself at the time, and I realized that my opinion of myself is more important than what other people think about me.*

Andrew's Mother: *He liked going to the group because he had boys he could talk to. He wasn't wanting to opt out of life anymore—I think he actually started looking forward to going to these meetings, and the boys there did talk to him, and I think he did like that. And I think he realized he wasn't the only kid in the world with issues. When you're a kid, that's all you know—you don't have any life experience to compare anything to.*

Little by little, Andrew left that scared little boy behind and started growing into the man he was destined to become. He even regained one of his old, bad habits.

Andrew's Mother: *He just kept getting better with things. I'd be like, "Um, you need to wash your hands now!" We went from one extreme to the other—there are times when you should wash your hands!*

It wasn't like I waved a magic wand and those other boys at school suddenly started behaving differently. As I mentioned before, the bullying was more about them and their issues than it was about Andrew. But the things they did and said to Andrew affected him less, because, inside, Andrew was different.

Andrew: *I didn't let it bother me anymore, and they picked up on that. There were still some bullies around, but it wasn't nearly as bad as it had been. After about a year or so, I didn't care at all what they thought of me. I didn't care one bit. I think they're just trying to feed off of people's misery. So once I let it stop bothering me, it came to a near standstill.*

This meant Andrew finally had the strength he needed to finish high school, graduate, and move on to a happier, healthier phase of his life.

Andrew: *I had a better opinion of myself. I had more self-confidence. I held my head up high. I made eye contact. I wasn't afraid to interact with people anymore, and I was able to be a better person.*

It has been several years since Andrew completed The Quest Project®. Now he is a young adult who has graduated from college and has a bright future ahead of him.

Andrew's Mother: *He talks more than he used to. He went through the police academy recently and I think that was probably one of the best things he could have done. Now I'm starting to see some social skills developing with the other guys that were in the academy.*

Andrew: *Ten years ago, if I talked to my younger self and told me what I was going to do, my younger self would be telling me, "There's no way. No, I don't see that happening."*

The boy who was bullied by other boys just finished a program where he was surrounded by other young men in a competitive, macho environment. Not only did he survive, he thrived—and he graduated.

What is it about the work we did in The Quest Project® that helped Andrew get to this place, when nothing else he or his mother tried seemed to help?

Andrew's Mother: *He (Clayton) didn't sit there and let them vent to him and then go home. He makes them face it. He gives them tools to deal with it and cope with it in the future. I think that's probably the key. I can sit there when something upsets me, and I can vent all I want, but if I don't know how to handle it, I'm going to shut down. He taught them that you don't have to shut down. He taught them: You cannot control what other people do, you can only control what you do.*

Andrew: *I left a lot of the hurt behind and a lot of the anger. I realized that if you hold onto those things, it can end up destroying you or making you less of a person than you already are. That's why I hold no ill will towards people that picked on me. We were in high school, we were kids, and we were stupid. That's our shit.*

In fact, today, Andrew sees what he went through as a child as an inspiration to help him work with other people using kindness and sensitivity that he could not access when he was a boy.

Andrew: *I've been the victim and I understand that it's a terrible feeling. I can empathize with that. I've lived through it. I think that will be a very big help in what I'm going to be doing as an officer.*

I like talking to people, I like interacting with them. I want them to know that I'm there to help them, that they should feel safe. I'm there to make sure that there's not going to be any harm that comes to them.

He has some words of wisdom for the kids who are being victimized or bullied right now.

Andrew: *It's hard not to take it to heart, but you're not going to see these kids again. You really shouldn't pay attention to what they're saying because teenagers can be ignorant. They really are. At some point, all that bullying and all that anger will eventually end. When you get out of high school, you move on. It's not going to be there forever.*

Instead, focus on your schoolwork, hang out with the friends that you have. Set goals for yourself. If you want to go to college, focus on getting the best grades you can to go to college. If you're out of school, focus on getting a career and make that your priority. Set goals and make sure that's your priority in your life then and there.

I'm proud of Andrew for everything he's accomplished, and I know there will be even more great things in his future.

Jordan

When is the right time to get professional help for a boy who is having problems? When you first suspect something might be wrong? Or later, when you have proof that he is in serious trouble?

There aren't a lot of hard and fast rules when it comes to parenting, and more parents than you might expect wrestle with this question. Pinpointing that fine line between "normal" adolescent behavior and behavior that requires intervention isn't easy.

No wonder so many parents wait until their son reaches the "completely out of control" phase or some sort of crisis before they take serious action. They don't want to be alarmist. They don't want to overreact. So they end up trying to live with the behavior, sometimes hiding their heads in the sand in denial, until their son gets in real trouble. While I truly believe it's never too late to help a troubled boy, I also believe it's never too *early* to ask for help if you suspect your son has a problem.

Meet Jordan.

Jordan's mother is the type who notices problem behavior early, in part because she became a parent when she was still a child herself. She made certain promises to herself about how she would raise her son.

Jordan's Mother: *I had him when I was seventeen. I always promised myself I would never lose my kid to any of the craziness that goes on.*

I have a fear that one of my kids, I'll find out that they're on heroin or something, if I don't catch it early enough. I got too scared and I became a control freak.

Jordan's father, who split from his mother while Jordan was still a toddler, didn't share this commitment to vigilant parenting. In addition to being an Absent Father, he was (and still is, although he's working on it) one of the fathers I talked about earlier who never got the guidance they needed to learn how to be a man.

> **Jordan's Mother:** *He [Jordan's father] took longer to become an adult, so he saw Jordan more when it was convenient—maybe once a month or once every few months. There was no consistency. Not that he doesn't love Jordan; he didn't have his priorities straight. But when he saw him, it would be more like, "We're buddies and we're going to play video games all night." It didn't have to do with the discipline part of it.*

Fortunately, Jordan did (and does) have a strong male role model. His stepfather has been a fixture in his family since Jordan was three.

> **Jordan:** *We've got a really good relationship. I've been through everything with the dude. He got me into sports and a bunch of stuff.*

The fact that he was growing up in a stable, loving family showed in Jordan's behavior.

> **Jordan's Mother:** *Jordan has never really needed discipline whatsoever. He's always been—you don't even have to tell him, he's just responsible for himself. I don't know why. Everybody who knows him will say, "How did you raise such a good kid?" I can't even take credit for it because, since he was a baby, he's always been easy going, people-pleaser, please-and-thank-you, always has regard for everyone around him.*

But then Jordan became a teenager. Suddenly, the cooperative boy who was never any trouble seemed depressed and withdrawn. He spent more and more time alone, locked in his bedroom—something a lot of parents of teenage boys experience and worry about. Because this was such a big change from the way her son previously behaved, his mother worried.

Added to the worry was the fact that one of her son's best friends was a known drug dealer. Both of Jordan's parents and his stepfather wrestled with past substance abuse and addiction. Jordan's mother did not want to see her son go down that path.

Jordan's Mother: *He went from the little boy who was the people pleaser, you could never imagine him doing anything wrong, very polite, never had to tell him anything, then all of a sudden he's a teenager with a mind of his own.*

When Jordan was just fourteen, his mother's worst fears were realized.

Jordan's Mother: *He's never been a follower, so I always warned him, "If somebody ends up talking you into something bad, they are going to brag about it until the end of time," and that's pretty much what happened. He tried marijuana, and word got around quick. It didn't take long for it to get back to me.*

Jordan: *I wasn't trying to show off. It wasn't peer pressure or anything; I make my own choices. I just wanted to do it for fun because people were talking about it. So I just tried it and that's how that went down.*

This was more than Jordan's Mother could handle. She—and the entire family—essentially freaked out.

Jordan: *It was emotional, definitely. My little brothers were crying, thinking I was going to go away for a while. And my mom was crying too.*

Jordan's Mother: *It was difficult. Very difficult. I was so angry with him that it took me a whole twenty-four hours before I could speak to him.*

Jordan's mother was angry for a reason. She had given her son everything she could, poured all of her energy into him with one primary goal, that he would not go through the same things she went through as a teenager. She was determined to protect him from making the kinds of bad choices that she had made. Now, he had made the exact same wrong choice.

She and her husband decided on a punishment that they hoped would teach Jordan a lesson and keep him on the straight and narrow from then on.

Jordan's Mother: *We had told him you will not do drugs. I will not live through that, and I won't watch you live through that, and I make that very clear. So right after that happened, we made him pack his bags, and we told him we were going to take him to his Dad's.*

And he didn't want to go—I expected he would want to, because he wanted the freedom, and it was a breath of fresh air to know that's not what he wanted.

So we told Jordan, "Okay, if this is the path that you are going to start going on, I'll promise you that you will end up in jail." He was grounded for a week, confined to his room except for showers and to go to school. We told him that this is what jail would be like—you get a bed and you don't even have a dresser in your room. He didn't have a phone, he stayed in his bedroom except to go to school, so when he went to school he'd come home, shower and get dinner, then go to his room.

After four days of this, Jordan said, "I know why you guys are doing this— you want to save my life." We did a lot of crying. After that, things went good for a while. And I really do truly believe that he wanted to do better.

But just six months later, Jordan's ten-year-old brother found an e-cigarette in Jordan's room.

> **Jordan:** *That wasn't peer-pressure, either. I did all of it by myself. My friend had one, so I got one and tried it out. Well, I had his first—we shared one and then it made me feel light-headed and stuff. I kind of liked that feeling of nicotine.*

And since he liked it, he kept doing it.

> **Jordan's Mother:** *I felt like I was losing control of him, losing touch with him. Like, "Wow, I don't even know who this kid is." Overnight, he wasn't this little innocent boy anymore.*
>
> *I immediately wanted to lock him in the house and never let him out again. I know I can't do that. I can't push him away. But in my mind I'm thinking, "I should have prevented it. It's my fault." And my husband, who has been through all of this, is like, "You're doing everything you can as a mom. You can't put him in a bubble, he has to decide things for himself."*

Then she learned that smoking e-cigarettes was only one of the secrets Jordan had been keeping.

> **Jordan:** *I didn't feel motivated to do any schoolwork or anything. I just wanted to go up to my friends' house and puff on the e-cig with them and stuff. I just didn't have any motivation.*
>
> **Jordan's Mother:** *On the same day I found out about the e-cig, it was parent-teacher conferences, and I got a report card, and there were three Fs and a D.*

When you discover your child has been hiding things from you, it's natural to wonder what else is going on that you don't know about. Jordan's mother knew about the e-cigarettes. She knew about the grades. And she knew Jordan had been keeping to himself more and more.

> **Jordan:** *I just wanted to be by myself and do my own thing. I didn't really care what my family wanted to do, I just didn't really feel like spending time with my family. I liked being around my friends and stuff, but not being around them.*

This made her wonder what other secrets Jordan kept. Was he smoking marijuana again? Or doing something even worse? It was upsetting and frightening. And like so many other mothers who realize that their son is in trouble, she didn't handle that realization especially well.

> **Jordan's Mother:** *Things were not pretty. I was saying, "Where's your mind?" and "What are you doing?" and even threw out, "Do you want to go live with your dad?"—which I admit was not the right thing to do. But I did. And he walked down the stairs and said, "I hate this family. I just want you to know that."*
>
> *I knew that wasn't my kid talking. I ran down the stairs after him and was so upset he said that, I said, "Look at everything you have and everything we give you! There are kids with a lot worse," and I even knocked his TV over because I was thinking, "You have a flat screen TV and a PlayStation and you don't work for anything!"*

> **Jordan:** *I felt like I really disappointed her, because after smoking weed and drinking and stuff I had her thinking I was good. And then I did that, and I got her all sad. I thought, "I screwed it up," and, "There's nothing I can really do but restart again."*

Jordan's mother knew enough to understand that if Jordan was going to restart, he needed help and she needed help to make it happen. It was not a problem she and her husband felt equipped to tackle alone.

Jordan's Mother: *I was getting more angry than anything instead of dealing with it. My expectations were so high, I left no room for mistakes. So I was like, "This isn't going to become a problem." The very next day I called our pediatrician.*

That's how she found me.

Jordan's Mother: *They gave me Clayton's number, and right away I called him and asked, "What is happening?" and he's like, "You're okay, calm down." So we made our appointment.*

By reaching out for help so quickly, Jordan's mother not only took control of the situation before it got any worse, she also gave herself some of the peace of mind she needed right away. Talking to a professional gave her clarity that Jordan could be helped, that there was someone on her side, that it was going to be okay, and that she had done the right thing.

Still, since Jordan had never seen a counselor before, she was a little nervous about the message she might be sending her son.

Jordan's Mother: *I didn't want my son to think I was taking him to somebody because I thought he was crazy.*

Jordan had his own concerns about seeing a therapist.

Jordan's Mother: *I just said, "We're going to see a counselor," and no, he wasn't crazy about it. He didn't know what to expect. He thought I was taking him to some rehab doctor thing, like you're lost and we have to* *find you and we're going to put you in a crazy house. He didn't like it at first, but he went, and he took it seriously when we had our first meeting.*

Jordan: *I obviously had that thought, "I'm not crazy or anything." I wasn't too psyched, but I just thought, "Okay, I'll do it."*

Once he saw that he was going to an office as opposed to a rehab facility, he relaxed a bit. From our first meeting forward, he approached the idea of going through The Quest Project® with a positive attitude. That might not have been the case if his parents had waited for something catastrophic to happen before intervening.

Jordan: *The only thing I had to change was to stop doing bad stuff and stop excluding myself from the family. Get my grades back up, of course. Being motivated and stuff like that.*

Jordan not only knew he had to change, he wanted to.

Jordan: *I was ready. I took it seriously. I took everything to heart.*

As I've mentioned before, one thing that makes The Quest Project® so effective to help boys open up and deal with their issues is that it shows them they're not alone. Being around other boys with similar issues takes the stigma out of being "in trouble." Jordan was no exception.

Jordan: *The kids that went in there with me all had problems. It was very comfortable because nobody could make fun of you. You had a problem, but they also had a problem. There wasn't any judgment. And since I was taking this (The Quest Project®) seriously, I was getting a head start. I was learning how to deal with stuff.*

That said, it's never easy for a fifteen-year-old boy to open up about his deepest, most personal feelings, even in a room full of boys like him. But once he realized that he was safe in the group, Jordan found that talking about himself wasn't difficult. The hardest part was worrying about what his new friends were going through in their own lives.

Jordan: *At first, I was nervous. As we went through, and on and on through the days of Quest, I wasn't that nervous, because I didn't have as many problems as the kids I was with. Even though my dad was absent, I still did have a father figure to raise me.*

Jordan's Mother: *He would come home feeling sad, but not for himself. There were some emotional times where he would get to crying, and I would only just say, "Everything okay? How did it go?" I wouldn't ask questions, but he would feel bad for the other kids in the meetings.*

Where I always tell parents that things will get worse before they get better, Jordan was an exception, possibly because of his strong sense of empathy.

Jordan's Mother: *It didn't get worse. I thought it might but that's not his personality. There were times when he would have an attitude but never lashing out. If anything, it got better because he made sure that he was aware of communication and things like that. He would say, "Mom, remember, I need my space too." So more like, he's teaching me things.*

As much as Jordan grew from his experience in The Quest Project®, his mother grew even more.

Jordan's Mother: *It wasn't easy. Clayton basically made me see that I pretty much had lost my little boy in a way—not in a bad way—but Jordan's not that little boy that I can control every move he makes. He told me, "You have to let go." And I cried. I've been so strong minded about, "You are going to be a great person when you grow up, and you're going to have all the opportunities and do all the things that I couldn't* do." But I've taught him, given him all the advice I think I can ever give him. It's going to be up to him to be smart enough to choose his path.

Through the work they both did through the program, Jordan developed a new, more adult relationship with his mother.

Jordan: *He [Clayton] taught me how to communicate with her, how to talk over stuff with her and stuff like that. I don't really make her angry or anything anymore. I'm not doing bad things to make her cry or anything. And we have a pretty good relationship now.*

I know that, even after reading this, you might not be inclined to seek help if you catch your boy smoking an e-cigarette. You might even let him off with a lecture if you learned he smoked pot for what he swears is his first and only time. Maybe, as you read about Jordan's mother, you felt she was overreacting. And it's true—a large part of what that family needed was for Jordan's mother to give her son the freedom to grow up and find his way.

But that doesn't mean early intervention is a bad thing. Parenting a teenage boy is almost always a challenge, and if your adolescent son doesn't seem quite like himself, or you suspect something is wrong but you're not sure why, seeking the right kind of help can only make the transition easier, both for you and for him.

Jordan's Mother: *I just knew whatever we were doing, I didn't know why, but it wasn't going to work. I didn't know why my lectures weren't going to work anymore. I just knew I needed to get somebody other than us who isn't going to judge him, because we are too biased.*

No one can say for certain whether or not Jordan was headed for bigger problems. We may never know what issues he was able to avoid thanks to his parents' early intervention. But we do know where he is now. Today he's on the path to a successful, productive life.

Jordan's Mother: *I don't think his situation called for a huge break-through. I jumped on it early enough that we didn't let it get to a situation that called for a huge breakthrough. We needed to shape the future.*

Jordan: *I feel motivated now. I don't really go down to my room by myself, and I'm not doing bad things anymore. I've got a goal now, to do good in school. To get good grades and earn my parents' trust back. That's pretty much it.*

That's pretty much all he needs to grow into a healthy, happy, successful man.

CHAPTER 11

Ethan

Helping a child who suffers from PTSD can be a minefield for parents. First of all, if your child has PTSD, you may not even know it, because the symptoms often look like other problems. Your son might have nightmares or experience depression or anxiety. He might show the lack of focus that leads (or has already led) to a diagnosis of ADD or ADHD.

Ethan had several symptoms. The one that concerned his mother the most was his intense, uncontrollable anger.

> **Ethan's Mother:** *It could be something as simple as, "Pick your toys up off the floor," or, "We're not going to have that for dinner," and it would set him off. His anger was so severe that he was actually scared of himself.*

Ethan's anger wasn't a complete surprise to his mother. She knew almost before it surfaced that there was more to her son's rages than a bad temper. Unlike a lot of parents whose children exhibit PTSD symptoms, Ethan's mother expected his childhood to be problematic almost from the beginning.

> **Ethan's Mother:** *We knew he was going to have issues. He's actually been in counseling since he was eighteen months old.*

Ethan grew up in a household where he was continually exposed to violence and abuse. A household where he never felt safe.

Ethan's father was an Iraq War veteran who served multiple tours of duty in the Middle East. When he returned from overseas, his rage was out of control. He screamed at his wife and yelled at his son. And the abuse wasn't just emotional. He'd pinch Ethan until he bled, but he saved the worst of his physical lashing out for Ethan's mother.

No child can witness this and emerge unscathed. Almost from the time he was born, witnessing and experiencing severe abuse was a regular part of Ethan's life. It affected him deeply.

> **Ethan's Mother:** *He had severe mommy anxiety, he wanted to be around Mom all the time. By the time he was four years old, he took a wooden dowel from a table and said he was going to kill his Dad. He told his sisters that Dad would never hurt Mom again.*

While the reason behind Ethan's rage was clearly his father, when it came time to choose victims for his own rage, everyone in his family was at risk.

> **Ethan:** *I used to have this metal truck and all these toys, and I would get mad to the point where I would throw them, and I would kick and scream. I got mad one time, and I hit my sister with a broom. I'm not really proud of that. I would also get mad every time they would try to "safe position" me. I would rip their hair; like, I ripped my sister's scalp one time.*

And the scariest part was, he didn't even realize he was doing it.

> **Ethan:** *I would get beyond angry—where I would black out and do things I don't remember. That's how the hair pulling and the broom hitting would happen. When I blacked out.*

As a result, while he was still very, very young, the authorities began to take notice of Ethan's behavior.

Ethan's Mother: *At six years old he was in a hospital for an evaluation against my will.*

Ethan's mother tried everything she could think of to help her son. She took him to doctor after doctor, hoping one of them would offer a solution to give Ethan and their family some relief. Unfortunately, when you bring a boy with behavior problems to the medical establishment for help, they have one very common (and I believe very misguided) way of dealing with it.

Ethan's Mother: *They advised many medications—Adderall, Ritalin— but I always felt there was a better way to do it, there was more than, "Here's medication."*

Time went on, Ethan got bigger and stronger and, without the right kind of help, even angrier. Eventually his mother felt she had no other options. She was terrified her child was turning into his father. She gave in.

Ethan's Mother: *He has an allergy to Adderall-based medications, so he was on Strattera and Louboutin.*

ADHD medications often have a tranquilizing effect on boys. Ethan was no exception. He hated the way the medication made him feel.

Ethan: *They would zombify me. I would always be drowsy, I looked like someone had just run over my dog.*

But even being drugged into a zombie-like state didn't make a difference when Ethan got angry.

Ethan: *It actually worsened. It actually made me stronger at times. Whenever someone made me mad, I would explode like a bomb.*

Ethan continued taking the medication in different doses, meeting with different doctors and therapists. His mother continued to search for a solution that would actually work.

> **Ethan:** *Whenever they attempted to help me, it only made it worse. I don't blame them. Their heart was in the right place; it's just, the meds didn't work.*

Nobody could give Ethan the help he needed.

> **Ethan's Mother:** *Nothing was working for him, nothing calmed him down. And he was starting to get bigger and it scared me to think puberty's coming and he's not even reached his full strength.*

Her son was not yet twelve years old, and she was afraid of him.

> **Ethan's Mother:** *When they talk about disabled people having special strengths, that's what it was like when he was angry. He would become so enraged that he wouldn't remember what he had done when he calmed down. He would look around and see the aftermath and ask, "Did I do that?"*

Ethan not only scared his mother with his rages, he scared himself.

> **Ethan's Mother:** *In the middle of these fits sometimes he would get scared and call out for me. But if I wrapped my hands around him, he would fight me.*

This boy, who loved his mother and wanted to be good and do what he was supposed to do, was being ripped apart by pain.

> **Ethan's Mother:** *He described his life at that point as being in the dark constantly. He begged me to kill him so it would be over for him, because he couldn't take it anymore.*

He told me he was the only one and he was a monster. And I told him I would love him so much, my heart would grow like a transformer and I would turn into whatever he was, just so he's not alone.

Unfortunately, love was not enough to heal the wounds behind Ethan's anger and pain. All the love in the world can't cure PTSD. And it wasn't enough to help Ethan.

Ethan's Mother: *He was aware that he could actually go to Juvenile for his rages, or into the psych ward.*

Ethan's father was transferred to a base in the St. Louis area. Shortly after that his parents split up. Ethan saw another psychiatrist in his new hometown. That doctor did yet another medication evaluation, trying to find the magic combination of drugs to make all of Ethan's problems disappear. To his credit, though, this doctor determined that medication alone not only wasn't working, it would not work for Ethan. He knew of another kind of treatment that might help Ethan get better.

He referred the boy to me.

I see a lot of boys who are tired of therapy, who don't trust that I can help them and don't even want to try. But after everything he'd been through and all the doctors who had failed him, Ethan still held out hope that maybe this time this doctor got it right.

Ethan: *I knew I would get the help, but I didn't know when.*

Ethan first met at my office with his mother. They told me about Ethan's uncontrollable rages, and they shared the long, painful story of everything Ethan had been through with his father. It was clear to me that Ethan had told this story many, many times before, and that the words he spoke were not even his. I asked his mother to leave so I could speak with Ethan alone.

I asked him, "Do you think I could help you?"

He started to cry.

I told him about The Quest Project®. I said, "By the way, I've got this cool boys' program. We have pizza and soda..." (The pizza and soda are always a big draw.)

> **Ethan:** *I was like, "Yeah, I guess I'll do it." And that's how all this happened. "I'll look into it." And then we looked into it a bit, and I was like, "Let's do it." I was psyched.*

A lot of boys I work with have some anxiety about joining the group and receiving "therapy" or "treatment" for their issues. But Ethan did not hesitate. He was ready to go, maybe because someone was finally offering him something different instead of pushing more pills at him. I was determined to find out what was behind his anger, so I could make it stop once and for all.

I don't know that I told all of that to Ethan. But I do know he had a sense that he had finally come to the right place.

> **Ethan's Mother:** *When he came out, he was so excited. It was a renewed faith. He said, "I think I can make progress with this guy."*

Once the program started, though, it wasn't quite that easy. Ethan had to deal with the same challenge every boy in The Quest Project® faces—he had to stand in front of a room full of strange boys and talk about things he had never spoken about to anyone except, maybe, his mother.

> **Ethan:** *It was very weird. I got stage fright, I cried a little bit. It was just nerve-wracking. "Oh God, I've got to open myself up. I'm not really used to doing this."*

Once he did open up, he learned the truth—that he was not alone.

Ethan: *There were kids who also had father figure problems. It made me feel sad, to know that their lives were worse than mine.*

Being part of the group and hearing the stories of boys like him helped Ethan feel comfortable opening up about his experiences with his father and the way those experiences made him feel.

Ethan's Mother: *Having the boys there sometimes gave him the words that he was trying to find to describe what he was feeling or what he needed to say.*

The positive effects of being in the group went beyond even that. Getting to know a group of boys who were also hurting helped Ethan to rediscover a part of himself that he didn't get to explore, having been labeled a "problem child" from such an early age.

Ethan: *My whole life, I've been wanting to help people.*

Eventually, Ethan would do just that.

But first, his primary task was to work with me and this group of boys to finally heal his pain and learn to cope with his PTSD. That meant confronting the source of his pain head-on, a process that led to very dark moods and difficult times at home. Those times weren't difficult only for Ethan. They were difficult for his mother.

Ethan's Mother: *Ethan had so many things come up, so many feelings and emotions. It was hard, because my baby was choking on them, and I just wanted to cuddle him up. I said, "I can't do this," and Clayton said, "Yes, you can. Something good will come. I promise."*

The most difficult week was when Ethan was challenged to get in touch with his anger and then do the scariest thing he could possibly imagine—let it out physically.

> **Ethan:** *The hardest thing of all was when we had to open our wounds up to heal them back again the proper way. That was definitely the hardest emotionally and physically, because there's a part of it where we would have this punching bag, and he would hand you a bat. Put you in your anger zone. I actually was very scared. I told Clay, I looked him in the eyes and said, "I don't know if I can control it."*

This was during the Anger Song exercise that I've written about in previous chapters. I knew Ethan needed to experience this exercise. Despite all of those outward expressions of rage that terrified his mother and his sisters, there was even more rage that he was holding inside. And beneath that, there was pain— pain from being raised in a home where he didn't feel safe, with a father who hurt him. If he was going to get better, he needed to confront that pain.

> **Ethan:** *He said, "Trust me," and I was like, "Okay, I'll trust you on this. You haven't failed me yet. I'll figure this is a good place to trust you."*

Ethan picked up the bat and let go.

> **Ethan:** *I got angry at my father because, no offense to him, he was the main reason.*
>
> *I almost broke the bag.*

The experience of being allowed to express anger at his father with no threat of repercussion, being allowed to confront the deepest source of his pain in a completely safe environment, was extremely emotional for Ethan.

> **Ethan:** *I came 1.2 seconds from bursting into tears.*

The Anger Song exercise is a highlight of The Quest Project®, because most adolescent boys are angry on some level—at being pushed away from their mothers and out into the big, scary world, at the very least. The majority of boys in the program have additional wounds that make the transition to manhood more difficult. Even the ones who don't seem outwardly angry benefit from the opportunity to touch their deepest feelings and let their anger out.

Ethan: *I felt very relieved. Of course, I was tired, but I felt very relieved emotionally.*

As Ethan progressed through the weeks of the program, his mother also learned better ways to help him deal with his anger. A family is a system, and when one part of that system (the boy) changes, the other parts need to change as well. Ethan's mother needed to learn new ways to deal with her son.

Possibly the biggest lesson for Ethan's mother was that her job wasn't to find a way to stop her son's anger, but instead to find a way to let him express it safely. This was a huge change since, in the past, she had been focusing all of her energy on trying to make Ethan's rage go away. Working with me she learned to let him have his feelings and process them in his own way, with some guidelines to protect his safety and the safety of the rest of his family and their property.

She only needed to provide a safe place, set the ground rules, and let him go.

Ethan's Mother: *Because it's my home, I can enforce everything that Ethan needs to do. If he's having a fit in the living room, everyone will leave him alone.*

Having that freedom to express himself when he needs to, knowing no one is going to try to stop him or shame him, has made it easier for Ethan to control his anger.

> **Ethan:** *Most of the time I like to confront it and try to talk through it, but if it's too much for me and I feel like Little Me is coming out, I'll say, "I need to go to my room." When we're outside, I'll go to the car and relax, or at my house I'll go to my room.*

As the weeks wore on, Ethan continued to improve. He became more focused. Eventually, he was able to discontinue all of his medication.

Perhaps most importantly, he relaxed and learned to trust himself. And he enjoyed the experience of being a part of the group.

> **Ethan:** *I looked forward to going, because (1) I got to have fun with them—we had funny conversations at times, (2) I got the help I needed, and (3) it was just a pure blast.*

In fact, Ethan participated in The Quest Project® multiple times. His parents were not always consistent about bringing him to meetings, so he stopped and started again the first time. Later, as an older adolescent experiencing other issues associated with growing up, he wanted to do the program again. He wanted help to process the new things that came up as he grew older, so that he could make a smoother transition to manhood.

> **Ethan:** *The last time I went was when I graduated. But in a way, you could say I came out as a young man during all of them.*

Since he knew the program so well, and since what he most wanted to do was help others, I invited him to work with me to help the boys in his group who were new to the program.

> **Ethan:** *The Younger Me felt like I was unneeded, and when he asked me if I could come back to help, that kind of made me feel like, "Yay, I'm needed for once."*

Today Ethan is very different from the sad, scared eleven-year-old who first showed up in my office.

> **Ethan:** *The Child Me was reckless. He was an angry little elf. He felt like no one loved him or liked him. He just wanted to be alone and he wanted to shut the world out. The Young Man me is, "Hey everybody, how y'all doing?"*

Ethan now has direction, goals, and every reason to believe he will reach those goals and become the kind of man he wants and deserves to be.

> **Ethan:** *When I graduate high school, I'm going to go to college and get a degree. Then I'm going to get a steady job.*

He credits his life turnaround to his experience in The Quest Project®.

> **Ethan:** *The number one thing I have that I learned the most is how to control my anger. But it also helped me mature, and it helped me realize the potential I really have.*

Ethan finally has the tools he needs to cope with his past experiences and live his potential to the fullest.

If you suspect your child is experiencing PTSD—for example, if he's having nightmares, raging anger, anxiety, depression, or has trouble focusing, or if he has been diagnosed with ADD or ADHD—there are ways you can help. The first is to educate yourself. Read whatever you can about PTSD and look for symptoms and signs in your son.

If you believe your boy fits the profile, find a therapist whose specialty is working with children who battle this disorder. It can be overcome!

Ethan is living proof that, with the right kind of help, there is hope of healing even the deepest wounds.

David

What is your greatest fear? The common answer from parents of boys entering adolescence is, "I'm afraid my son will start using drugs." Parents know drugs have the power to derail a young man's future and to steal his motivation, his ambition, and in some cases even his life.

For David's mother it wasn't just a fear, it was her reality. But as with so many parents in the same situation, she did not recognize that reality right away.

David's Mother: *I really thought my eyes were wide open as far as a using kid and the signs; but he was hiding the obvious signs I might have noticed.*

David's mother was sure she knew her son well and that she would know if he were using mind-altering substances. She was positive she would recognize the signs. This is not uncommon. Parents don't understand how determined kids are to hide their drug use, and how creative and sneaky they can be. David's drug use had escalated to the point where he was selling marijuana before his mother realized that he was using.

David: *I was really outgoing before I started to use. I guess she noticed I stayed inside all the time, didn't want to go hang out and all that stuff.*

David's Mother: *I noticed that his grades plummeted, and he was defi-nitely skipping school. He was sleeping a lot, and he also lost interest in playing sports. He had always played sports—every sport.*

The good news is, once her suspicions were aroused, David's mother did the right thing. She was lucky enough to have a family member who was uniquely qualified to help, and she reached out to him immediately.

David's Mother: *I knew David was having a difficult time, and I called his uncle, who is a therapist and also a drug treatment counselor. His uncle knows him very well. He said, "Sounds like he's doing a lot of drugs. Do you know?"*

She didn't know yet, but she was about to find out.

David's Mother: *He recommended we go to an outpatient treatment center. I told David we would be doing that, and he agreed, and so we went to a local center, and he spoke to the treatment manager there, and he came out and talked to me, and we had a meeting. He said, "Do you know how much David is using?" and I said, "I have no idea." That's when I realized he was smoking pot. I wasn't shocked by that, but I was a little bit surprised that he so readily admitted it and said it was why his life was in shambles. That was odd, in a good way.*

David's mother saw his honesty as an indication that his drug use was a cry for help. Rather than hide it, he opened up and admitted drugs were affecting his life in a negative way. Like so many adolescents who turn to drugs, David used them to self-medicate. He was living with pain from a wound he had no idea he had or how to heal, and marijuana was his only way to make that pain go away.

David: *It just makes you feel good. That's the main reason why anyone does drugs and gets addicted to things. It takes you away from reality.*

David's pain had been with him for a long time, at least since he was seven years old, when his parents divorced. I don't blame parents who get divorced, and I don't advise anyone to stay in a bad marriage. I've been divorced, and I know it's a fact of life. But don't underestimate the trauma of the split for your children.

David's Mother: *It affected David. He would write about it sometimes, and every once in a while he'd give me some of the writing to see. It was very intense—poetic prose, written in a poetic format, expressing that he was upset and that he was angry.*

Once she knew how David was suffering, his mother tended to her son's pain.

David's Mother: *I tried a thing called "Kids in the Middle," a support system for kids whose families are going through a divorce. I got them a little involved in that just to get them new outlets and possibilities to talk about what they may or may not be feeling. David hated it. The other brothers liked it—they didn't love it—but he just abhorred it. Would turn chairs over and refuse to talk to me. It was very clear.*

I think he was just mad. He was hurt and sad. It was like, "I didn't sign up for this. I hate this, so I'm going to let everyone know how much I hate it."

What David's mother didn't know at the time was that her son had wounds even deeper than his parents' divorce. What she did know is that he had always been a handful. David is a triplet and has a reputation as the rowdiest of the three brothers.

David's Mother: *He was harder to discipline. For instance, he would not sit in a time-out. He would not sit in a chair for five minutes. When he was four, I put him in his room because he wouldn't sit in a time-out chair. I said, "Go in your room," and I went back into the living room, and as I was sitting there looking out the front window, I saw David running with a big smile on his face across the front yard. I was like, "Oh my God."*

He had climbed up on a dresser and he had managed to open this big window and push out this giant screen, and then leap from the window, which was a good five feet off the ground. For a four-year-old, that's kind of a scary jump. But he leaped out. Got away. He was happy about that.

In addition to the two brothers he shared a womb with, David has three other siblings. Like other kids who grow up in big families, he did not want to get lost in the crowd. From an early age David had special ways to stand out.

David's Mother: *When they were little, David would always be the kid who took the other kid's food or the toy. He was that guy. Extremely curious. There was a day where we had little sippy cups on the table, and he was able to toddle around the table and at one point was like, "Mom, look at me!" He had two sippy cups, one in each hand, and he proceeded to show me how he could drink out of both sippy cups at the same time. He said, "Mom, I can drink from two cups at one time."*

While David's mother thought his behavior was cute and precocious, his father was more critical. That criticism intensified as David got older.

David: *My dad was saying stuff like, "You're lazy," and, "You're not going to be going anywhere. You're going to be a bum when you're older."*

One of the most common wounds I encounter in young boys is the wound that comes from the absence of a father's unconditional love. This is the wound David did not know he was struggling with, but it affected his behavior from an early age.

> **David's Mother:** *His temper, even before the divorce, he just had this crazy temper. He could be highly emotive, so when he was mad he was flipping-out mad. Screaming. He still doesn't have a door in his room; I'm not gonna replace that.*

Eventually, like so many boys with similar issues (and so many of the boys I see in my practice and program), David wound up in a therapist's office. Before long, he was on medication for ADD. But the medication did not solve his problems.

> **David's Mother:** *He got worse with the divorce. He expressed more anger toward his father. As he got older, he may have written more about that as well. The feelings changed.*

Knowing this, it's no surprise that when David was exposed to marijuana, he used it to numb his everyday pain. He retreated, hid in his room playing video games, did not interact with anyone or anything. His behavior clearly bothered his family, but no one realized that David suffered from depression.

> **David:** *I wanted to hide away from reality and what was going on around me. Wanted to push it all away and didn't want to hear any of it.*

> **David's Mother:** *He wasn't really hanging out with his brothers (the triplets). They were getting more angry with him, because they're like, "What are you doing? You just sleep." Berating him really hard. He was sneaky, but he would sometimes lie about things.*

His personality just became dulled a little bit; he wasn't participating in life as much as he used to. He'd make excuses about it, but the teachers at school would say, "We started to figure out that we could tell if he was coming into class high because he would put his head down."

That meeting with the counselor at the treatment center was the confirmation David's mother needed that something was wrong. When the counselor suggested she enroll David in the center's outpatient treatment program, she agreed.

David: *He suggested that I go to the rehab place. He just said it was like a program, and I was like, "Sure, whatever." I just decided to go do it.*

David's Mother: *They had a great treatment facility that was newer for adolescents and teenagers. It was the summer after freshman year. They would come pick up the kids every day and take them to the facility and then drop them back off in the afternoon. When school started he had a few weeks left in the program, so they just did a few afternoons in the week.*

David completed the program and was able to stay away from drugs most of the time.

David's Mother: *He did a pretty good job staying clean; not perfect, though. I can't say he had a sober date and kept that sober day. He had a few relapses.*

Whatever David accomplished in rehab was not enough to take away the pain that triggered his drug use. He also took multiple prescription medications, including drugs for ADD and drugs to control his impulse to smoke marijuana.

The drugs made him gain weight. He had no energy. He was no longer a habitual marijuana smoker, but beyond that, he was not much different than he had been before rehab.

David: *I was just kind of drifting in between things. I really didn't feel like doing anything.*

That's when the outpatient program counselor recommended that, as a next step, David come to see me.

David: *I wasn't too keen on the idea, but I didn't hate the idea either. I was like, "As long as it's not the shit I was doing at rehab, I am totally fine with that."*

In reality, David wasn't totally fine. Between the medications and the time spent in the outpatient program, he was tired of treatment, and he was even more tired of talking to people who were supposed to fix what was "wrong" with him. He didn't believe I would be able to help him.

David: *I was like, let's get this over with and move onto the next thing. That's definitely what I thought at first, because that's usually what would happen. The same shit, just presented differently.*

When David's mother brought him in, I got a clearer view of why David was so resistant to treatment. She spent almost the entire hour of our first session listing all the terrible things David had done, in great detail. I let her talk until the end of the session, but then I said something I don't think David expected. I said, "You talked about how bad he is. What do you like about him?"

Then I turned to David and asked, "Why don't you come back and I'll let you tell your story without Mom sitting here?" That was the beginning of a bond of trust between David and me.

My intention isn't to insult David's mother, or any parent who reaches that end-of-the-rope point with their son. I see frustrated parents in my practice every day. It's my job to help them and to help their boys. One thing I strive to clarify for the parents, because my goal is to help them, is that when they constantly berate their boys and only focus on the negative, it makes things worse.

Telling your son what's wrong with him is one of those "don't be" messages I mentioned earlier in this book. It adds to whatever pain is behind his bad behavior. That makes it even harder for him to change or get better. Even worse, it sets him up for a lifetime of depression.

I felt David was headed down that road the first day he came into my office. It was my job to prevent him from slipping further into depression.

My first step was to build trust with David and forge a relationship with him. After a few one-on-one sessions, when we had established enough of a bond that he might be receptive, I told him about The Quest Project®.

> **David:** *He said, "We have this boys group, you're welcome to be a part of it." And I was like, "That'll be cool. I'll see what that's about."*

Looking back, I remember that conversation a little differently. I remember David telling me he was tired of groups and had no interest in joining mine. He also told me he was nervous about being in a group setting with other boys. But I told him about the pizza and soda (always my big selling points), along with the most important thing—if he didn't like it, he could quit.

He agreed to give it a try.

When the time came for his first meeting, David was still feeling the effects of the impulse control drug he'd been taking. He showed up late and acted out to get attention.

> **David:** *I was putting on a front to get a feel for what's going on. But I think everyone does that for a while to get comfortable with the people in the group.*

David acted up because he was afraid to talk about himself in front of the other boys. He was afraid that they would judge him. But he soon learned that he was wrong.

David: *At first I was a little hesitant. Everyone was. But I got comfortable with the people in the group, and I didn't have a problem sharing because they had similar situations. I could relate to them, so I wasn't alone.*

Once he felt safe in the group, he opened up to the entire experience of The Quest Project®.

David: *In the beginning I still had my doubts, but then I realized, "This could actually help me," because it was a change of atmosphere.*

However, the kinds of changes boys experience in Quest can sometimes lead to drama at home. As David uncovered the source of his pain, he got angrier and angrier at his parents.

David: *I think it was more my dad than my mom, just because he was the one telling me what to do, and I was like, "Shut up," and I didn't want to hear it.*

His mother, however, was ready for it.

David's Mother: *He had always been so in touch with his inner anger and never had any problem expressing that, that I didn't really notice heightened behaviors that I hadn't already dealt with.*

Instead, she noticed improvement, nearly right away, as David got down to the business of addressing his pain.

David's Mother: *He was definitely able to come to a place where he was identifying aspects of his father that he had not been willing to look at or* *deal with and articulating that he found those things unacceptable. "My dad did these things, that's not okay, I'm not putting up with his crap anymore." The way his father had treated him and spoken to him—he wasn't going to put up with it.*

As the weeks went on, David started shifting his focus to what it meant to grow up and what he wanted to do with his life.

David's Mother: *I saw him being willing to talk about his future and being willing to stay clean and willing to talk about it and be more motivated and willing to go to school and not miss the bus every day. Those kind of things were happening.*

But moving to the next step would be difficult for David. When he was using, he had fallen so far behind in school that he wasn't expected to graduate. The tools he learned in The Quest Project® helped him stay in school and get his diploma.

David: *It did help me graduate. I wasn't really motivated to do anything other than just sit around and do nothing. He (Clayton) helped me focus on turning my shit around, so I could actually be something and not a dropout.*

I thought I wasn't going to make it. I think other students really didn't think I was going to make it either, but I showed them. I ended up pulling through at the end. I went there and graduated. It felt awesome to do something people thought I maybe wasn't going to be able to do.

Graduating from high school was only the beginning of David's plans for a successful future.

David's Mother: *He's been saying he's been wanting to go to the military for a while. That is motivating him—he wants to join the Air Force. Part* *of him realizes that his grades weren't good enough to get scholarships, but if he goes in the military they will pay for college.*

For a boy who did nothing except smoke pot and play video games to now plan a future with the military and college is a significant accomplishment. I'm proud that The Quest Project® was a part of that.

David: *I immensely enjoyed going there and talking with the guys and Clayton. It was a way to go and talk about what was going on with us and get rid of that built-up frustration. I really enjoyed that the most.*

When I asked David why he thought The Quest Project® worked for him when the other therapists and medications and treatment programs did not, here's what he said:

David: *It really feels good to be around other people who understand you for who you are and being able to share with them things that you normally wouldn't share with other people.*

David's mother sees it this way:

David's Mother: *David needed a positive male mentor who was not going to berate him, who made it safe for him to look at these things that were painful and that hurt, and being able to identify it and root it out.*

I was happy to be that mentor for David, and I'm proud of the fine young man he has become.

CHAPTER 13

Steven

I've given a lot of air time to Absent Fathers and the toll they take on the boys I work with and on adolescent boys in general. They are, by far, the most common problem I deal with every day.

But occasionally, I will work with a boy who has neither a mother nor a father to provide him with the love, support, and stability he needs to grow into a healthy adult.

Steven was one such boy.

When Steven first came to see me, he was seventeen years old and the kind of kid society typically dismisses as a lost cause. He was flunking out of high school. He had been in and out of trouble since preschool, including several stints when he was hospitalized because of his aggression. He even spent time in juvenile detention. He had seen dozens of doctors over the years who said he had ADHD, and since he was a kid who didn't talk to people, they also diagnosed him with Asperger's Syndrome. He had been prescribed a lot of medication.

But there wasn't a medication that existed that could cure what was hurting Steven.

Steven's Grandmother: *His mother had a lot of issues. I love my daughter, I don't want to say she's a bad mother, but she often thinks more of herself than other people, and it's always a "poor-me" attitude.*

She got married three times. After the first marriage, she came and lived with us for a while. They moved out when she moved in with what ended up being her second husband. She was here, she was gone, she was here, she was gone. I wanted to put a revolving door on the front because of the times that she moved in and out.

Steven, along with his older half-sister and, eventually, his twin half-brother and half-sister, joined their mother as she moved from place to place to place and from partner to partner. He constantly changed schools and left friends and started over. He saw his mother use drugs, and he witnessed her abuse by her romantic partners.

Still, every time a new man came into their lives, Steven held hope. Maybe this would be the one to finally offer him the stability he so desperately wanted.

Steven's Grandmother: *When Laura would get married or when she'd move in with somebody, he would ask that man, "Can I call you dad?"*

He got along with some of the men better than others, but Steven never found the father figure he was looking for.

Steven: *When they did move in, I knew it was kind of a serious thing, so I'd get attached to this person—much easier than I should have. And then they'd be gone. It was one heartbreak after another.*

As for his own father? He did even less to show Steven that he mattered.

Steven's Grandmother: *His father is very rarely in the picture. Steven doesn't get Christmas cards or presents, he doesn't get birthday calls or presents or cards or anything from him.*

Growing up for Steven was hard and painful. Without a father in his life and with a mother who (though she loved him) was unable to put his needs before her own, Steven never received the guidance, support, or direction he needed. He never learned how to behave or to cope with pain and disappointment.

Steven never felt as if he mattered.

Like so many boys whose parents are not there for them, he soon emerged as "the problem child."

> **Steven's Grandmother:** *Steven always showed anger. He was asked to leave four preschools because of anger. Between the age of seven and, I would say, ten or eleven, he was hospitalized five times.*

> **Steven:** *With my anger, when it happened I blacked out. And then I'd wake up and be like, "Oh my gosh, what happened? Why did I do this?"*

During his angry blackouts his behavior was extreme.

> **Steven:** *It was third grade, and I ran away from school. I don't remember why I was mad anymore. And, when I was running, the principal chased me to try to track me down and get me. Prior to that, we had a camp-out out in the field and I picked up one of the stakes we used for the camp-out and I stabbed him in the leg with it.*

> *I was a little kid but I felt really bad and I sent him an apology card.*

If you are a grandparent or caregiver for a child like Steven who hasn't had the love and support he needed in his formative years, you may recognize this kind of behavior, especially if that child is a boy. And you may have no idea how to deal with it, let alone control or stop it.

I want to stress that this type of behavior is not the child's fault. It does not mean the child is a lost cause or that he can never be taught responsibility. In fact, the opposite is true: taking interest in a child like Steven, listening to him, helping him work through his issues, and most importantly, showing him he matters, may be the only way to save him.

It's certainly the best way.

Steven mattered very much to two people in his life who provided the stability his mother did not. Steven's grandparents (his mother's mother and her husband) offered him a safe place to stay when life at home was too hard. They opened their doors to his mother and his siblings when she was between partners and had nowhere else to go. His grandparents were the one constant, stable influence in Steven's life, and he could turn to them whenever he needed them.

> **Steven:** *One night I was asleep, and my mom's friend Beth—who was her girlfriend at the time—came over drunk to the house. I woke up to my mom getting the shit beat out of her in the living room. I had to call the cops. It was bad. I walked all the way from Saint Anne to Bridgeton to sleep at my grandma's house, and I was about twelve.*

Unfortunately, when Steven was thirteen, he lost the option of escaping to his grandparents' house when things at home were intolerable. His mother found a new man and moved across the country to Los Angeles, taking Steven and his siblings along. Soon after they resettled in California, Steven's grandfather, the only strong male influence in his life, passed away.

Steven lived his teenage years thousands of miles from the only person who ever took the time to care for him. He lived with a mother who offered no stability, who stayed out all night and drank too much, and a man who abused her. It was like Steven had no mother at all.

Sometimes he had to be the adult in the relationship.

> **Steven:** *I was sixteen. I didn't drive, so I'm walking at one o'clock in the morning to go pick my mom up from the bar because she's drunk. I was*

going to go walk her home. I mean, it's a good ten miles walking. I was about six miles away and I get a text from her that says, "Hey, I got a ride from two guys—you can head home." And then it turned out that she had to stop at a gas station because these guys were going to try and rape her.

Steven's mother gave her son no reason to listen to her or regard her as an authority figure. He had to make his own rules. He also stayed out all night, sometimes just to escape what was happening at home. As he got older, he got angrier, and his mother couldn't handle it.

Steven's Grandmother: *She always a hard time disciplining him, because she believed he had all these different problems, because that's what the doctors told her. As he got older and bigger—because he is six foot tall and one hundred and eighty pounds, and his mother is five-two and one hundred and twenty pounds—she was afraid of him.*

She was right to be afraid.

Steven: *Me and my mom used to have problems. We'd butt heads as I grew up, and it just got way more heated. One night she was drunk and I was taking these classes to help control the anger. They'd tell me to just head to my room and leave the situation. Well, she was in the way. It just turned violent and I blacked out and then I beat the hell out of her.*

I woke up, figuratively speaking, and I called the police on myself. I told them to come get me. That happened the first time.

It would not be the last time.

Steven: *The second time, I was laying on the couch, and I wanted to get our dog, who would run out of the house all the time. She ended up sitting in the way, going, "Don't go get that dog." And she threw the coffee* *table at me, and that's when I blacked out. And I called the police again. And that's when my grandma said, "I'm going to come get you."*

Steven's Grandmother: *He was put in juvenile hall. The day he was released from juvenile hall is the day I brought him back to St. Louis.*

Now this angry, out-of-control teenage boy was his grandmother's responsibility. But unlike her daughter, she wasn't afraid to lay down the ground rules.

Steven's Grandmother: *When we were on the plane coming back to St. Louis, I told him, here's the way it's going to be. You are not going to act the way you did in California. You are not going to be out 'til all hours of the night, because I'm going to be home, and you are going to be there with me. I gave him guidelines: this is what you are going to do. He didn't have much of a problem with that.*

Steven: *I was a little upset because it wasn't as much liberty as I had out in California. But at the same time, I understood why she did it.*

Maybe it was because, for the first time in a long time, Steven felt like somebody actually cared about him. And he didn't want to lose that.

Steven: *Juvenile Hall was never an option. I didn't drink or smoke, I respected my family.*

But with the damage caused by his unstable childhood and the medications he took and the fact that no one ever taught him the lessons a boy needs to learn growing up, the odds were still stacked against Steven. His grandmother continued to seek a solution.

Steven's Grandmother: *His doctor, his psychiatrist suggested that he see a counselor. Because the psychiatrist talked to him, gave him his medicine, but he never had the time to sit down and delve into stuff.*

There was a counselor near our home, in Bridgeton, and I took him to her. That lasted a couple of times. He didn't feel comfortable.

Steven tried to control his temper on his own. He managed to lose control only, as he puts it, "sporadically." But one of those sporadic outbursts landed him in trouble again.

Steven's Grandmother: *At school, there was a girl that was giving Steven some problems. And Steven blew up one day.*

Steven: *I was eighteen. I punched a hole through the window at school. It was a shatterproof window—it had wires and stuff through it.*

Steven's Grandmother: *It cut his hand all up. Afterwards, I was talking to his counselor at school, and I said, "I've got to find something else for this boy. There's gotta be something out there, someone out there that can help him."*

The counselor recommended she bring Steven to see me.

Steven's Grandmother: *I asked Steven, do you want to try this gentleman counselor, and he said, "Yeah, maybe I would be more comfortable with a man."*

Not that Steven was entirely happy about it. After what must have felt like an entire lifetime spent in and out of psychiatrists' offices, hospitals, counseling, and other programs, he had reason to be skeptical that another therapist would be able to help him. But he agreed to give it a try.

When we talked, maybe because I listened to what he had to say and didn't label or judge him, we established a rapport.

Steven's Grandmother: *When we left there, he said, "I like him," and I told him, "I'm glad, that's important."*

When I told him about The Quest Project®, he trusted me enough to agree to try that too. Like most of the boys I work with, though, he was sure he wouldn't feel comfortable talking about himself in front of a group of strangers.

> **Steven:** *I felt like I would have not said a word. Like I would have just sat there awkwardly, just listening. I felt like it was going to be one of those groups where it was like, "I'm Steven. I'm an angry guy."*

When he arrived at our first meeting and experienced what The Quest Project® is actually about, he relaxed.

> **Steven:** *It was welcoming. We had relaxing furniture to sit on.*

Maybe because it was different than he expected, or maybe because the group was made up of boys just like him, he surprised himself and opened up at our very first meeting.

> **Steven:** *Awkwardly enough, I spoke up pretty big the first day.*

In that room, with other kids like him, Steven felt safe and less alone.

> **Steven:** *Because all these boys—I went in there, I thought they would be like, tattoos, doing drugs—that was not at all the case. One was a golfer who lives with a very rich family, one was a football player. I didn't at all expect them to be this normal.*
>
> *But you could tell that they hid it. Just as much as I did.*

In The Quest Project®, Steven found a place he could be comfortable enough to be himself. This is essential for a boy who wants to heal the wounds in his life and figure out what kind of man he wants to be.

At the same time, Steven had a lot to overcome. His parents' complete failure to make his needs a priority meant his wounds were very deep. I advise parents that it's going to get worse before it gets better. This was especially true for Steven's grandmother. I knew I needed to prepare his grandmother for difficult times.

Steven's Grandmother: *Things were going along pretty smooth, and then all of a sudden it was like somebody flipped a switch. I knew that was when it was getting worse.*

He became rather angry. There were different outbursts—there were times that I told him, "I'm not your mother, and you're not going to talk to me that way." But then he would go talk to Clayton, and things would be better.

Clayton was addressing the issues with moms and dads and that type of thing, so I thought, "Okay, Carol, you gotta just step back and think about this."

I rode it out, and it started getting better again.

Steven: *He brought up these emotions in the group that almost seemed locked away. He used the problem and attached the emotion to it and funneled the emotion out of—I don't want to say my soul, you know when you have a wound, you get cut, you have all this kind of bad blood in there? It's almost like he irrigated the blood inside of this wound and all this bad blood came out of this wound and then the wound healed.*

As he moved through the weeks of The Quest Project®, Steven learned to deal with negative feelings that he had buried deep down inside himself in order to survive. It was painful, but he finally accepted that the way he was treated as a child had nothing to do with him, that he was not at fault.

Steven: *I went through this program expecting it to be an issue like that, and it turned out that wasn't. It was just a burden that I was putting on myself—and I shouldn't have.*

More importantly, he learned that he didn't have to grow up to be like his father—or his mother.

Steven: *I felt like Steven. I felt like who I needed to be.*

Because of that, he was able to change.

Steven's Grandmother: *He changed a lot. He seemed calmer and more focused, especially in school.*

Once he started believing in himself and seeing himself as something other than "the bad kid," Steven realized that he could choose his own future and decide what kind of life he wanted to live.

Steven's Grandmother: *He told me, "I'm taking charge of my life." Now he's doing better in school and looking forward to June because he's planning on going into the military. He has a direction. I can see that working on him now, and I can see him working toward that.*

None of this would have been possible without the dedication of Steven's grandmother, who was there for him when he needed her and never gave up trying to find him the help he needed.

Being called upon to take care of a grandchild or other child who has been neglected or abandoned is a special responsibility, and not an easy one. Children in Steven's position are likely to be troubled in one way or another, which is an extra challenge when you're parenting the second time around, when you may have less energy than you did for your own children.

Every case is different, but this same advice applies to nearly all grandparents (and can be modified for other relatives or friends) who take on this difficult and crucial role:

- Get legal guardianship of the child. This entitles you to health benefits for him (or her).

- Benefits are available for grandparents who are raising grandchildren. Check with your local Department of Family Services (DFS) to find out what you qualify for.

- Ask the DFS to appoint a school advocate for your grandchild.

- Research the many other organizations that assist grandparents who are raising children, and review the services they provide.

- Find a skilled counselor who specializes in this issue.

- Read, research, and learn as much as you can about how to raise a healthy, happy young man.

Remember, you now are wearing two hats, your grandparent hat and the parent hat. You have taken on one of the toughest, more thankless jobs out there. You should be commended.

The parent job takes precedence, and you will need to wear that hat most of the time for your grandson's sake. Schedule a day once in a while to take off your parent hat and be the grandparent you deserve to be (and he deserves to have).

As for Steven, he is preparing to graduate from high school next year and take his next life step. Even though he was nervous, he took a test to enter the military. Since he had never done well on tests, he worried about failing.

It turned out he had nothing to worry about.

Steven: *I had an above-average score. I had every branch in the military contact me about my score and talk about interviews.*

Today, not only is Steven in demand, he's choosing his own future and deciding, for the first time, where he wants to go and what kind of life he wants to live.

> **Steven:** *I won't do Air Force, Navy, or Coast Guard, because I don't like boats, but I want to delve into the Marines or the Army. I'm probably going to go into the Marines.*

Rather than being a burden on society, he is preparing for a life that's all about giving back.

> **Steven:** *I didn't see myself serving my country—being this person that I always dreamed of being.*

Steven no longer takes ADD medication. And he's pretty sure he does not have Asperger's Syndrome. All he needed was for someone to help him see that, despite everything he had been through, he mattered.

Because he does.

CHAPTER 14

Sam

Most parents don't expect adolescence to be an easy time for their children. Incoming messages from media, from society, and from other parents warn them to strap in and prepare for a bumpy ride that will start in middle school and last well into high school.

In my expert opinion, those warnings are well founded.

Adolescence is a time of major transition and turmoil for both boys and girls, and parents are right to expect behavior that is, at the very least, different from what they've experienced up until that point. There will be anger. There will be mood swings. It comes with parenting a teenager.

However, the fact that unusual behavior is expected doesn't mean parents should dismiss it as "just a part of growing up." Sometimes that behavior indicates that a child is depressed.

Depression in teenagers, particularly boys, can be tricky to deal with. The challenge to distinguish between normal adolescent mood swings and something more severe, especially when boys aren't open about their feelings, is tough for parents. More often than not, if you ask a teenage boy if something's wrong, he'll tell you everything is fine.

Even if it's not.

It's crucial to talk to your child, to notice changes and take appropriate action. Failure to act can be devastating. Suicide is currently the second leading cause of death among people aged ten to twenty-four, and of the reported suicides in that age group, the vast majority (over eighty percent) are male.

Sam may have been headed that way.

> **Sam's Mother:** *He was at his Dad's house, and I was at home. My niece texted me and said, "Hey? Where's Sam? You need to check on him. He just texted me saying, "I'm sorry for...whatever I've done, blah blah..." Saying stuff that a person who was about to commit suicide would say, like, "Nobody is going to have to worry about me anymore."*

> *My ex was on his way home. I got to his house, and he had gotten there. I can't remember who called who, but the cops ended up coming and basically said, "You have to take him to a hospital, otherwise we are going to call an ambulance."*

This wake-up call took Sam's mother by surprise. Until that night, no one had noticed anything unusual happening with Sam.

> **Sam's Mother:** *He never showed signs of depression like moping around or staying locked up in his bedroom or not eating or sleeping all the time.*

Sam's mother had been hyper-aware of her son's ups and downs from the day he was born. As the result of a doctor's mistake, Sam came into the world before he was ready. His mother expected problems from that very first moment.

> **Sam's Mother:** *I was told by one doctor that my due date was wrong and that I was farther along than I was initially told.*

Thinking she was overdue, Sam's mother was hospitalized and labor was induced. But the baby was in no hurry to be born. When he finally was born, it was clear to the doctors that he had, in fact, not been overdue and that he had been brought into the world before it was time.

Sam's Mother: *The experience was traumatic. They used the vacuum— I think that's what caused some of his eye problems. When he was born he had a hemorrhage in one of his eyes. He's extremely far-sighted, which causes one eye to overwork while the other eye starts getting lazy. He's overly sensitive to stimuli, and so as an infant and toddler he was very fussy and cried all the time.*

As Sam got older, those issues intensified.

Sam's Mother: *He would just throw himself down on the floor and scream and scream. Not like in a grocery store when a kid throws a tantrum, if you'd swat them on the butt once they'd be quiet. If you'd swat Sam on the butt once or twice, he'd scream for half an hour.*

Since she believed her son had been damaged during the birth process, Sam's mother didn't think there was anything she could or should do to control his behavior.

Sam's Mother: *I remember being with a bunch of family at Christmas, and he was acting up—but he was only two and a half. One of my cousins said, "If that was my boy, I'd tan his hide." I was just like, "Yeah, well, you don't realize that's going to make him explode through the roof and make the situation even worse."*

Without the right kind of guidance from his parents, who expected him to have problems and thought there was nothing they could do about them, Sam didn't learn to control his emotions.

Sam's Mother: *He'd throw things. He hit himself in the head. It was over the top— "I am hurting, and I am going to do everything I can to make it hurt more."*

The trauma of her son's birth blinded Sam's mother to the possibility that other things may have contributed to Sam's pain. There was, in fact, at least one major factor. Like so many of the boys I see in my practice, Sam grew up with an Absent Father.

Sam's Mother: *When he was born, his dad was in the military. There were times when he was gone for weeks at a time, then he'd come home and basically sleep. Didn't do much with us. When he got out of the military, he went straight into transportation, which kept him away from the house all the time. When he took time off during the vacation days, he'd go on camping trips or fishing all the time, but he only took Sam on one or two trips. In fourteen years.*

Sam developed deep scars from not being a priority in his father's life. Still, despite the anger he expressed when he was little, by the time Sam got to elementary school, he seemed to have outgrown that anger on his own. In school he was known for being quiet and shy, but he still had some behavioral issues. His mother discovered that he had been stealing from his classmates.

Sam's Mother: *I was finding all kinds of stuff in his room. I was like: "Where did this come from?" I literally collected a grocery bag full of stuff and took it back to the school. And I gave it to the teacher and said, "I'm sorry." When he got older, he stole money from his cousins.*

The cause for stealing seems so simple. We assume children who steal take things because they want them. But stealing is not so much about the items kids take, but about the people they take them from. Stealing from a person is how some children attempt to connect themselves to that person. When they steal something from someone, they have a piece of them, and that secures an opportunity to see that person again.

While stealing is fairly common with kids, it can indicate a deeper issue. In Sam's case issues were expected, so Sam never saw a counselor about it. Eventually, he outgrew it, just like he outgrew his anger.

> **Sam:** *I just figured out that it was wrong of me, I guess. As a kid I didn't know that much. As I got older, I was like, "That's kinda bad."*

When the stealing stopped, everything seemed fine. Sam's mother had no idea that Sam was hiding feelings deep inside that provoked him to steal and triggered his anger of before. His feelings never went away. Instead, Sam turned his pain inward, as do so many boys. It's what I did when I didn't get the love I needed from my dad. I didn't act out; I became distracted and unfocused.

That's what happened with Sam.

> **Sam's Mother:** *I would tell him to do something: take this and put it here. And he'd take it and walk five steps, turn around and say, "What was I supposed to do with this?" There was one time my ex gave him some papers and said, "Go put this by my bowl"—the bowl he would throw his keys and stuff in—and he later on went to throw something away and it was in the trash can.*

Like so many other boys, the only "mental health treatment" Sam received in his first fourteen years was a prescription for ADD medication.

> **Sam's Mother:** *It was so bad that I was afraid for his safety. He was old enough to ride his bike without me being there the entire time, but I couldn't let him do that because I was afraid he would not be paying attention if a car was coming.*

He took the medication for two years, and it worked for a while. But as he got bigger and his dosage changed, suddenly there were side effects. At that point his mother took him off the drug, and he was able to stop without any issues.

When Sam turned fourteen, his world changed dramatically. His parents split up. The split was an angry and difficult one, and at one point Sam's mother got a restraining order against his father. Sam missed his dad and had a hard time dealing with the situation.

> **Sam's Mother:** *The depression set in when his father and I split up.*

> **Sam:** *I was upset with my mom that I had been taken away from my dad.*

Sam's mother realized her children might need help processing what was happening. She took Sam and his sister to see a female therapist in their area.

> **Sam:** *I wasn't against it, but I didn't really like it, because I didn't know what it was. I just felt like there was something wrong with me, and that's why I had to go.*

Whatever was "wrong" with Sam, talking with the therapist didn't fix it.

> **Sam:** *It wasn't helping at all.*

> **Sam's Mother:** *There came a point in time when he was like, "I don't want to go back. I'm tired of talking about everything. All it does is make me feel worse." I said, "If that's the case, I don't want you to go either." I didn't want him to feel worse, even though you have to feel worse before you get better. At the same time, I didn't see any progress at all.*

The therapy ended after a month or two, and since Sam never caused much trouble, no one paid heed to his mental health again. Until that night when he was fifteen, and his mother received a text from her niece saying that Sam might be suicidal.

The good news was, Sam had not made a serious attempt to take his life.

Sam: *I think it was just that I wasn't trying to kill myself; it was me taking my anger out on myself.*

Sam's Mother: *He didn't hurt himself. He used a razor, and he just scratched his wrist a little bit, but didn't actually cut like cutters do. It was more like a cry for help.*

The hospital staff agreed, and after meeting with Sam's mother and father and talking to Sam, they determined he wasn't a suicide risk. Sam was allowed to go home with his mother. She immediately set about finding a new therapist who could help him get to the bottom of whatever was causing him so much pain. But Sam didn't want to talk to another counselor.

Sam's Mother: *He was resistant. "I told you I don't want to talk about it anymore." I said, "Well, this is different. It's a guy. It's a man this time, not a woman."*

That man was me.

Not that Sam was at all interested in meeting me.

Sam: *I didn't want to go. It was like the whole ordeal with last time; I already knew what was going to go down, and I didn't want to go through that again, because last time I felt like it didn't help me at all. And it didn't.*

Sam's mother insisted, and once he talked with me and saw that I wasn't there to "fix" something "wrong" with him, Sam agreed to give me a chance.

Sam: *He came off really cool, not like everyone else. He knew what was going on, and he just kinda wanted to help me.*

When I told him about The Quest Project®, he agreed to try it.

> **Sam's Mother:** *He talked to Clayton a few times over the couple of weeks before the group started, and it helped him establish a rapport between them.*

> **Sam:** *We talked about doing a group session, and I thought maybe that would help me more.*

Agreeing to join the program when it was just me in the room was one thing. When it came time for his first meeting to talk about himself in a room full of strange boys, Sam was nervous, just like most of the boys I work with before they meet the group for the first time.

> **Sam's Mother:** *Initially he was nervous and didn't want to do it, because he's a reserved kid.*

> **Sam:** *It was really sketchy to me. I didn't like the idea of sharing in front of people.*

Once he met the group, he felt safe enough that he was able to open up. As the weeks wore on, talking in front of the group got easier.

> **Sam:** *I was more of the quiet one. But that changed over time after I got to know them a little more.*

> **Sam's Mother:** *After the first few times he got to where he felt like, "This isn't so bad," and he wanted to go.*

Hearing the other boys sharing their stories of feeling hurt and acting out helped Sam understand what so many boys need to know—that he was not alone. Other boys like him had problems, too.

> **Sam:** *I didn't feel really normal, but like, "Okay, well I'm not the only one who goes through something like this."*

For Sam, those other boys turned out to be the best part of the experience.

Sam: *I can admit that I had a lot of fun. It almost felt like I was getting to just hang out with them and talk out everything, rather than what felt like being interviewed.*

But The Quest Project® is much more than just hanging out. It's hard work, and some of that work proved to be a bit of a challenge for Sam.

Sam: *When we had to close our eyes and imagine things, because it was something that was very new to me, I didn't understand it at all. We did it twice. Once I imagined my hate, and once I imagined my future self.*

The exercises felt strange to Sam. Most of the boys who have gone through The Quest Project® don't have much experience with visualization. But the visualization exercise gave him a way to uncover, confront, and deal with feelings that he had kept bottled up for years.

Sam's Mother: *I know Clayton said: "It's going to be really hard, they're going to be dealing with some issues." But he never acted differently. There were times when he would talk a little bit more about what they did, and then there were times where he wouldn't say anything. He would just want to play music on the way home or whatever. And there were times he was really excited because, "I got a pizza," or, "We did this!"*

It wasn't long before Sam's mother noticed her son changing for the better, in ways she never expected to see.

Sam's Mother: *He was more motivated in school. Just happier overall. He would come home and he'd talk to me and tell me all the stuff about his day and ask me to do things and stuff like that. Whereas before, he would just come home and go straight to his room and close himself up for the rest of the day.*

For the first time, Sam felt that he had value, that he had something to offer the rest of the world.

> **Sam:** *I felt like I was accomplished, like I knew what to do to get through some of the stuff I was going through. How to cope with my emotions.*

Sam grew so much over the course of the program that his mother wasn't the only person who noticed the change.

> **Sam's Mother:** *I've had teachers tell me, "Sam's great! He motivates other students to do what they need to do and stuff like that." He's talking to more people, he's not just all clammed up like he used to be.*

Working with other boys like himself in The Quest Project®, Sam not only found a way to heal the wounds that blocked his happiness and success, he found strengths and talents he never realized he had. It is because of those strengths and talents—not the story of how he was damaged at birth—that he can now look forward to his future, see how to become the kind of man he's meant to be, and live the life that he wants to live.

> **Sam:** *I have a better sense of what I want to do when I'm older—when I get out of high school—now. My job, or if I want to have a family later on in life. I want to go into engineering.*

We don't know what would have happened to Sam if he hadn't received treatment for his depression. But we do know that today he is a happy, confident young man on his way to a productive life.

And that's what matters the most.

According to the Mayo Clinic, these are symptoms of teen depression:

Emotional changes

- feelings of sadness, which can include crying spells for no apparent reason

- irritability, frustration, or feelings of anger, even over small matters

- loss of interest or pleasure in normal activities

- loss of interest in, or conflict with, family and friends

- feelings of worthlessness, guilt, fixation on past failures, or exaggerated self-blame or self-criticism

- extreme sensitivity to rejection or failure, and the need for excessive reassurance

- trouble thinking, concentrating, making decisions, and remembering things

- ongoing sense that life and the future are grim and bleak

- frequent thoughts of death, dying, or suicide

Behavioral changes

- tiredness and loss of energy

- insomnia or sleeping too much

- changes in appetite, such as decreased appetite and weight loss, or increased cravings for food and weight gain

- use of alcohol or drugs

- agitation or restlessness—for example, pacing, hand-wringing or an inability to sit still

- slowed thinking, speaking, or body movements

- frequent complaints of unexplained body aches and headaches, which may include frequent visits to the school nurse

- poor school performance or frequent absences from school

- neglected appearance, such as mismatched clothes and unkempt hair

- disruptive or risky behavior

- self-harm, such as cutting, burning, or excessive piercing or tattooing

If your teenager shows some of these signs, talk to him about what he's feeling. It's okay if you don't know the right thing to say. No parent does. What's important is that your son knows that you are there for him and that you care. And it's important to use your best judgment to determine if your son is coping well with his feelings. Bear in mind that he may not tell you everything.

If you think your child may be depressed, don't wait. Make an appointment with his doctor or talk with his school counselor or a local mental health resource center as soon as possible, with the goal of finding a qualified mental health professional who specializes in working with adolescents. Depression does not get better on its own. Be sure your son gets the treatment he needs.

Finally, if you worry your child may be suicidal, call a suicide prevention hotline immediately. All talk of suicide should be taken seriously, even if you think it's not. Reach out to your son's doctor and/or school counselor, as well as friends, family, and community members for help and support.

CHAPTER 15

Joey

I n the past few chapters you've witnessed the powerful impact that fathers have on their sons' lives. The father/son relationship is crucial as a boy transitions to manhood, giving him a sense of who he is as well as who he is capable of becoming in his growth from a boy to a man.

When that fundamental relationship is flawed, the boy suffers.

Absent Fathers damage their sons through their absence. By not being there to provide guidance for their sons, they inadvertently send messages like, "You're not good enough for me to spend time with;" "You don't matter;" and even, "You'll grow up to be a screw-up like me." Such messages are devastating to a boy trying to find his place in the world. But even fathers who are present and dedicated to their sons sometimes send messages that destroy, especially when they focus primarily on the negative.

Joey's story demonstrates this.

At first glance, Joey is the kind of teenager other boys wish they could be and the kind of son you'd think most fathers dream of. He's a top athlete in his area, scouted by colleges and organizations who see his future in professional sports. It looks like he's living the dream.

But for Joey, life has been more of a nightmare.

Joey's Mother: *His dad was extremely hard on him. Had high expectations. He saw it as, his father didn't push him so, "I'm going to push* *my kids so they can be bigger, stronger and better." He watched all these athletic shows that had all these professional athletes, and they'd thank their parents for pushing them. So he was going to push his kids. He was living through his boys.*

At least in the beginning, Joey did not live up to his father's expectations.

Joey's Mother: *Joey felt like he wasn't loved as much—nothing he did was good enough.*

Joey: *I was overweight, I wasn't good-looking. All the kids made fun of me. I was just the one kid that no one liked and was picked on all the time. I'd walk around all pissed-off, mad, upset. No one wanted to hang out with me or be my friend.*

Joey's younger brother was the son that made his father proud.

Joey: *My brother—he was considered the born athlete, the one that's the superstar. He gets all the straight-As, everyone likes him, he's a popular kid. My dad always looked at him as the golden child. He didn't favor me. It was always my brother.*

Joey's father took that favoritism too far.

Joey: *When I was nine or ten years old, my brother ended up punching my youngest brother, in the face, so I broke them up. But my father thought it was me fighting them; he picked me up by my neck and started choking me. He was honestly about to kill me—the room started fading out and I was like, "I'm going to pass out," so I had to punch him to make him let me go.*

The relationship became so toxic that Joey was afraid to be alone with his father.

Joey: *He would get in my face all the time and yell at me. And the scariest thing—it might not seem like a big deal to most people—but when it happened to me, face-to-face, he would squat down, put his hands on his knees, look me straight in the eye with his sunglasses on and then slowly take them off. When he'd take them off, it'd just be his eyes staring straight at you. Like, "You do that again, you will regret it."*

You never knew with him. One day he might be nice and happy, and the next day he'll be about to kill you. I never knew what was going to happen, and when my mom was gone—she was my protection; if she was there, I knew I was safe.

Too many times Joey felt unsafe. His grandmother, who lived in another state, was sick, so frequently Joey's mother was gone to take care of her own mother. In her absence, Joey's father expected him to take over for her.

Joey: *He would make me do everything around the house. I would have to cook for the whole family. I'd have to clean the whole house, I had to do everything. And if it wasn't perfect, he would make me do it all over again. He'd get mad if his food wasn't perfect or if it wasn't just how he liked it. "No. Do it again. I don't like it."*

I wouldn't go to bed until—the earliest, two o'clock and the latest four o'clock. I'd get home from practice around eight, have to cook, clean, and all that, then I'd do my homework and go to bed for a few hours and have to wake up, go to school, and do it all over again.

The constant pressure and lack of support from his father eroded Joey's already fragile self-esteem. By the time he was twelve, Joey had left the overweight boy behind and developed into a top athlete. But outside of the game, he felt like that boy who couldn't do anything right. Perhaps because he still saw himself that way, his peers also viewed him as the same kid they'd always picked on, but with a new twist to accommodate his new, fit physique.

> **Joey:** *I'd walk down the hallways and people would call me "Steroid Joe" because I was bigger than everyone else.*

It was hardly the life you'd expect for a sports hero. Instead of being popular and respected, he was ostracized.

> **Joey's Mother:** *Freshman year of high school was a hard year. He'd come home and say, "Everyone hates me. No one likes me." In a notebook with nothing else in it I found this letter to no one in particular and from no one in particular. This letter was, to me, somewhat of a cry for help from someone. I remember reading it, and this person was "feeling like they're going down a black hole." I was like, "Is this Joey?" I called the school counselor because I did not know where to turn. I did not know if this was Joey, but it was in my house.*
>
> *I didn't hear anything back for days. I asked Joey about it. He denied it; it wasn't his. He did not write it. I believed him. Nothing else came of that.*

He may or may not have written the letter, but Joey was suffering. His mother had no idea how much he suffered, because he was not comfortable opening up about what he was going through.

> **Joey:** *My father taught me, "If you have nothing good to say, don't say anything at all: Real men don't show their emotions." So he always got on me if I ever showed my emotions and told me to keep things inside, that no one wanted to hear my problems. I kept everything inside; I was convinced that no one cared how I felt, or even if I told someone that they'd just judge me for it. I was judged all my life.*

At school the situation worsened.

Joey's Mother: *Shit was written on the wall about him; they would make fun of his voice, because Joey had a really deep voice. The kids would mock him, make fun of him. It sucked.*

He wouldn't approach to talk to anybody. He would always wait for someone else to talk to him. He'd look down at the floor.

Joey: *I was so depressed and sad. I felt like there was no point in life; I was so depressed. I had no friends, and no one was nice to me. I didn't want to do anything. I'd come home pissed off, mad, upset—so stressed. I wouldn't get sleep. I couldn't do anything. Then it all started overwhelming me. I was always the person keeping my problems to myself.*

As much as Joey kept things to himself, he did open up to his mother about some of his problems. While she was sympathetic, she also expected him to have some issues transitioning to high school. She had heard other parents mention the "freshman funk," and she assumed whatever was wrong with Joey was normal.

That changed when things reached the breaking point with his father.

Joey's Mother: *I was on one of my trips—I wasn't even gone for a day. Joey's like, "Mom, come home." I couldn't, because my mother had just had surgery. I had to have Joey removed from the house because he was scared to be there with his dad. He went to my girlfriend's house. She took him in for the three days in which I was gone.*

When Joey's mother came home, she decided something had to change.

Joey's Mother: *That was the straw that broke the camel's back. There's a lot more going on here than I'm aware of. Here I have a young man who doesn't seem to have a healthy relationship with his dad, and that's not* normal. He's having a hard time at school, at home, he doesn't feel like he has any friends.

She decided to take Joey to see a counselor, and she searched for someone in her area. The first two names on the list were from her insurance company, but in both instances the appointment fell through. Time passed, and she thought maybe it was okay to let things lie.

> **Joey's Mother:** I dragged my feet and I dragged my feet. You think you're open to it, and then it's you and it's like, "Well, he seems to be doing okay..." And then in tenth grade, again, he didn't want to go back to school. I thought, "Wait a second, something has to change. This will repeat itself. He needs to find his voice and his strength."

My name was next on the list.

> **Joey's Mother:** He inquired as to how I found him, whether I was familiar with The Quest Project®. I'm like, "No, I never heard of it. But, oh my God, this was meant to be. There's a reason the first two didn't work out. I was led to you. Awesome."

In Joey's opinion, getting professional help was anything but awesome.

> **Joey:** I didn't want to talk to someone about my problems that I didn't know. I felt uncomfortable and I really didn't want to do it.

His mother convinced him to come to my office and meet me. We met one-on-one, with the ultimate plan being to get him into The Quest Project®.

> **Joey:** At first it was a little hard. It was very emotional, and it was hard getting everything out. But once it all started coming out, it became easier but, at the same time, very nerve-wracking. Until the next few times I went, then it became easier and I felt more comfortable.

Joey's Mother: *Clay made him feel so relaxed and so comfortable. There was this rapport built; he made him feel at ease and relaxed. Joey felt safe talking to him. We just did one-on-ones for a while. Just a safe place for him to go and work through whatever he needed to work through at that point in his life.*

We knew that the ultimate goal was to find that peer group for Joey. To know that "it's not you." Like, you think it's you and it's just you, and that you're the only one feeling this and experiencing this. You're not alone. You're not crazy. This is normal. This is part of this journey. It's how you handle it and how you come out on the other side.

But when I mentioned The Quest Project®, Joey would shut me down. Not only was he worried about being in a group with new kids, he was also worried that he might already know some of them through athletics.

Joey: *I didn't want to do it at first because it was me talking to other kids. Maybe not my age, but ages close to mine. Not sure if I, for some reason, would end up knowing them or not. I felt like they'd think I'm weird or messed up, and they'd judge me.*

I knew it was what he needed. So I kept pressing.

Joey: *Every time he brought it up, he'd say, "Talk to your mom about it." I said, "All right." I'd say a few words about it but then I'd say I didn't feel comfortable about it. She's like, "Okay, just give it some time." Clayton kept bringing it up and I finally agreed with it.*

When the day finally came, Joey was nervous.

Joey: *I was very scared. It was hard to talk. I'm not the person that likes talking in front of people, because I'm afraid of being judged and everything. I've never been good at talking well. As a kid, I always had* *trouble reading and some problems talking. It wouldn't come as natural as it would for some kids. On top of me being afraid, not all words would come out as I would think them—it'd be harder for me to say them.*

The Quest Project® is designed to be a safe place. And it didn't take Joey long to realize that part of the reason he could be comfortable being himself was that the other boys in the program were a lot like him.

Joey: *It made me feel like I wasn't alone; that I wasn't the only one that I felt this way. Everyone at my school seems happy, they're always with their friends, talking, laughing. I'd be walking alone in the hallway feeling like no one wanted anything to do with me. Seeing that I wasn't the only one that felt that way was relieving.*

Like most of the boys who go through Quest, Joey quickly became comfortable with the group and the food and the relationships that developed between the boys. The exercises, however, which are designed to provoke some discomfort by forcing boys to confront their pain, were a bit more challenging.

Joey: *Probably the hardest thing was the visualization thing. He had us go down deep and visualize ourselves climbing up a mountain, and then seeing this barrier that was our fear keeping us from our goal and what we wanted to be. My barrier was water, because that's one of my biggest fears, water, when I can't see or feel the bottom. It terrifies me. That was, in the way, acting as my biggest fear. Also the trap where I can't do any-thing on my own—my father dictating my life is me stuck in the water, and I can't get out, because I don't know what to do, because I'm afraid and I'm panicking.*

Getting through that exercise was challenging for Joey, but at the end was a reward for his hard work. Not only was Joey able to see that he was stronger than he believed, he also unlocked the mystery of why he had been in so much pain for so long.

> **Joey:** *After doing that visualization, I felt so much more relieved and I could see my fears and my problems so much clearer. I could see what has been holding me back and everything. It all became so much easier and clearer, as to why I felt that way and what I have to do to overcome it. That it's just an obstacle.*

When I realized how much damage Joey's father had done, I shared with him some of my experiences with my own father. Hearing an adult professional who he respected talk about similar experiences helped Joey understand that the way his father treated him had very little to do with him and everything to do with his father.

> **Joey:** *He (Clayton) told me it was not my fault—I did not bring this upon myself. I had no control, but all I could do was be the bigger man and learn that it's okay to embrace your anger and your fear. Just don't let it control you. Even though it sucked at the time, time passes, and before I know it, I'm an adult and my own person—I already am—where I don't have to deal with any of it.*

Once he understood that his wound came from his father and he was able to stop blaming himself for his pain, Joey left it behind and blossomed into the young man he was destined to become.

> **Joey:** *Before, I felt like I was so down and dark. I felt heavy—everything was so bunched up inside me. As the program went on, I felt lighter and lighter. It went from dark and heavy to light. I felt a light, I was seeing everything more clearly. All of this just coming out, for once, just felt so much better.*

Joey's Mother: *He's able to have a conversation now. He's able to have a smile that might open up the door to have a conversation. He took a job at the place where he worked out, cleaning, maintenance, bottom of the chain. Simple. But he took such pride in that, in his name and his job. He would talk to people and engage in conversation. He just kind of came out of this shell.*

As the program continued, Joey made a crucial decision. He decided that, if he was going to live a healthy, happy, and full life, his toxic relationship with his father had to end. And he had to be the one to end it.

Joey: *I told him to leave me alone, that I wanted nothing to do with him because of how bad he's hurt me over the past ten years of my life. Treating me the way he has, I wanted nothing to do with him. The last time I talked to him was almost two months ago. I have nothing I need from him, and he has nothing he needs from me.*

It was a brave thing for a young man to do. However, in Joey's case it was also the right thing, because now, freed from his father's constant, negative influence, he is finally fully able to grow and thrive.

Joey: *I'm happy, for no reason: I don't even have a reason to be happy. Instead of me being mad and upset all the time, I'm happy all the time because I'm so stress-free. All of this just coming out, for once, just felt so much better.*

Joey's Mother: *He's quite a young man. He was more of a shell of a young man; he's a strong young man. More confident. He's smart, he's intelligent, he's confident—not that he wasn't before, but people stand up and take notice in a different way because he can stand there and have a conversation.*

If you met Joey today, you might not believe that only a year ago he had no friends, he felt he could do nothing right, and occasionally he even felt life was not worth living. Instead, you would see him as a young man with a happy life.

> **Joey:** *Everyone's so much nicer to me. The kids who used to never talk to me, I walk down the hall and they say, "Hi," ask how I'm doing and everything. They talk to me. It's totally changed. Everyone is now nice to me, they talk to me, I have no problems.*

Joey's success isn't just about feeling happier. He has also grown in ways neither he nor his mother expected when he first came into my office.

> **Joey's Mother:** *He has grown up. This was the one thing I wanted for Joey. There's still room for growth here, but there has been a huge difference: owning it. Taking responsibility for yourself. With insecurity, always trying to put something off on someone else—now, it's his maturity, his ability to do it.*

Joey's maturity extends to his plans for his future. As a top athlete, college scholarships and even the prospect of playing professionally have been real possibilities. But there are no guarantees in sports, and Joey suffered a knee injury last season that may affect his playing career. Currently recovering from surgery, Joey knows that how his recovery progresses will determine whether he continues to hold the attention of the scouts who have been so interested in him.

While this type of setback might devastate another young athlete, Joey is taking it all in stride. In fact, he already has a "Plan B" in place that he is excited and enthusiastic about.

> **Joey:** *I just took the ASVAB test three, almost four weeks ago.*

Wherever the future may take him, Joey will be ready. Having overcome his obstacles and having learned what he's learned, he feels prepared for anything life might throw at him.

I asked him what advice he has for other boys who feel alone and isolated the way he did.

> **Joey:** *I was in the same place as you once. Everyone feels that way sometimes in their life. Some have the courage to overcome it by themselves and stand up and be the bigger person and prove everyone wrong. And for some other kids it's harder. But no matter what, don't lose faith in yourself, because it all works out.*
>
> *You may not feel that way. I didn't feel that way when it happened to me. But now as I see through the darkness and through my pain, there were always people there for me. They might not have shown it or came forward, but as time went on I could see how the whole time they were there—even if they weren't there physically, they were there mentally, watching out from afar. Making sure I was okay. They were there helping the whole time.*
>
> *As you mature, it will all come into place and work out. Everything's a lot better in the future.*

I am honored and happy to be one of those people in Joey's life. I was deeply touched when I received this essay he wrote for school.

> *Clayton is not only my therapist and my hero but he is also my friend. A few months ago I started going to Clayton because of some problems I was having with bullying, making friends, and my father. Thinking I was going to hate it right away and be afraid to talk about my problems because I'm not the most open person about my prob-*

lems. I'm the kind of person who likes to keep everything to himself, not wanting to be judged.

But as time went on and seeing Clayton once a week I started to notice this man I just met is literally just like me. We have the same interests, same hobbies, when he played sports back in high school he played the same sports as I did. And also this man was in the Air Force and not just one of the guys who enlists and is deployed for a few months and goes into something else. No, this man was a captain in the Air Force, all the time when I would go in to see him we would always get talking about the military and he would tell me stories. Like there was this one time where he was just laying low at the base waiting for the special ops guys to arrive and it is pitch dark and then out of nowhere these guys come out with these glow sticks in their mouths. And I recall him saying, "it was like they were marshons [sic]."

Yes we had our fun telling stores and everything but it always wasn't fun and games when seeing him. He actually dug down deep to find the problem he didn't just talk about everything and then act like he knew what he was talking about. He helped me go face-to-face with the issue and not only confront it but also take it in and let it all go. Along with all of that anger and fear that has built up for the past 10 years.

The biggest inspiration he has ever done is when I told him I wanted to go into the military and suggested Air Force. Yeah that probably would be the best bet for me but I didn't want to go into the Air Force, I want to go into the Marine Corps and actually fight. People think I'm crazy. They think I have a death wish or something, no I just want to be able to fight because I haven't been able to my whole life so far.

Clayton might not seem much to you but he's my hero and that's all that matters to me.

Joey
September, 2015

Having that kind of impact in a young man's life, to help someone who feels desperate or unloved or alone to find strength and passion and happiness—that is the best part of what I do.

CHAPTER 16

Moving Forward

I hope that meeting some of the boys who have completed The Quest Project® has given you hope for your own son's future. These young men are living proof that even the most troubled teenagers can go on to lead successful, productive, happy lives. With help, your son can too.

I also hope that this book provided you with tools to understand what your son may be experiencing now, as he transitions from boyhood to manhood. I hope you've come away with concrete ideas of what you can (and can't) do to help him grow into the healthy, responsible man he's meant to be.

It's your turn to take the next step on this journey.

If you don't know where to start, first let go of the Fantasy Son you dreamed your boy would become. From this moment forward, accept and appreciate your son for the person he truly is. That is the person who needs your help growing from a little boy into a man.

Next, use some of the exercises in this book to set boundaries and set natural consequences for your son's behavior. Use the exercises to open up the lines of communication, resolve conflicts, and begin to heal your relationship.

It's crucial that you engage a healthy, male mentor, whether it's your son's father or another man he trusts, to help guide him through his transition to manhood. Reach out to men in your community who can offer their own perspectives and support.

Use the information in this book to assess how well your son copes with the challenges of adolescence. If you sense that he is struggling and needs extra help, use what you've learned to find the right therapist or program for him.

Find your own therapist to help you navigate your emotions and the challenges you face as the parent of an adolescent boy.

Continue to read, study, and learn everything you can about teenage boys. And know that this, too, shall pass.

Raising a teenager is the most challenging stage of the adventure known as parenthood. Now you understand the reason these years are so tumultuous. Trading the safety of childhood for the great unknown of manhood, while at the same time developing his own identity apart from his father, is a painful process for a young man.

There is no more important time in your son's life. It is crucial that you be with him now.

The young men you met in this book overcame obstacles, discovered their potential, and are building bright futures despite the odds. They did not get where they are today solely because they worked with me. They got there because they had parents who cared. While those parents made mistakes, they didn't let things lie, or turn the other way, or simply hand their boys some pills and hope for the best. They didn't give up, and they didn't stop trying until they found something that worked.

They might be a lot like you.

My final piece of advice is to keep doing what you're doing by staying involved, interested, informed, and by continuing to learn. You don't have to be perfect. You just have to be a healthy example, and you have to be present.

Help your son through this transition now, and you will ensure he has the potential to become the man he wants to be. Whoever he wants to be.

He can do it. And so can you.

CHAPTER 17

A Little about Me

E arlier in this book, I mentioned my own difficult childhood and the struggles that came out of that. I explained that I work with boys who are hurting because I was a boy who hurt. Now, before I leave you, it might be helpful for me to tell you a little more of my story, so you can understand where I come from and why I've chosen the work that I do.

I grew up the oldest of three kids in a working-class family in suburban St. Louis. Our dad was a former Marine-turned-blue-collar-worker, as well as a classic example of the "Absent Father" I introduced earlier in the book. He was an alcoholic who also physically and mentally abused my mother, my siblings, and me. Much of my childhood was spent moving back and forth between our home and our grandparents' house as my mother packed up the kids and left my father over and over again.

My childhood was no picnic. I had very little support or stability, and I carried the painful, damaging knowledge that I was not a priority.

Unlike many of the boys I work with, I wasn't the kid who got in trouble. I didn't act out, because I feared my father and his rages. My survival mechanism was to avoid provoking him at all costs. I worked hard to keep my siblings in line, and I spent a tremendous amount of energy trying to fly under the radar. Because of my PTSD and my unstable home environment, I did poorly in school, and I was a bed-wetter until about nine years of age, which is common with kids from chaotic households. Overall, I grew up with a strong sense that no matter what I did or how hard I tried, I would never be good enough.

In retrospect, I was lucky that I was afraid to get into trouble; this is not uncommon in children who do not feel loved or wanted. I lived with fear every single day. I was more at the quiet and unhappy end of the spectrum than the boy who is loud, acts out, and calls attention to himself. As I got older, I began to self-medicate with alcohol, and I turned to girls for the love and attention I didn't get from my parents. I became obsessed with the way I looked, to the point of being narcissistic.

When I was a freshman in high school, I told my father I wanted to be a doctor. His response was, "Forget it—you're not smart enough." My parents finally split up for good during my senior year in high school. In an attempt to "go out with a bang," my mom burned our house down. My four-month-old puppy died in the fire along with a lifetime of childhood memories, some good and some bad. Soon after that my girlfriend, my first love, broke up with me. I was lost. I attempted college, but I had no real direction and no idea what I wanted from the experience or what might interest me. Eventually, I dropped out and joined the Air Force, which turned out to be a perfect fit for me.

The military dynamic was ideal. It was like having another father to perform for and please, except this father was consistent and rewarded me when I did well. That consistency, combined with the knowledge that I could perform to somebody's expectations, inspired me to push myself hard. I excelled, my confidence grew, and when my tour of duty was over, I went back to college and got an engineering degree. I was invited to become a commissioned officer in the Air National Guard, on track to become a General.

However, my career success did nothing to ease the pain from my childhood that was still buried deep inside of me. And that pain wreaked havoc. I still drank to numb the pain. I married twice, both times for the wrong reasons, and cheated on both of my wives. I ended up with two divorces, a boatload of heartache, and no idea how to have a successful romantic relationship.

Through circumstances beyond my control, I lost my job in the military and my dream of becoming a General. I went back to school to study marketing, since I needed a new way to make a living. I also fell into a deep, depressive funk from which I could not escape.

That's when I discovered therapy.

Having someone give me an opportunity to talk about my feelings and my problems and sort through them felt good. I was so impressed with what the process did for me that I changed my major to psychology and studied everything I could get my hands on. My goal was twofold: get my degree and heal myself.

Healing, it turns out, is a journey. It doesn't happen all at once. Over a two year period, I concentrated my energy on healing the little boy who never got the love he needed from his mom or his dad. I learned that, in order to heal, I had to find a way to nurture myself, to give myself the support I never received from my parents, and to silence the critical voice inside me that told me the things that happened to me as a child were my fault. I researched how healing worked and, with the assistance of my therapist, put myself through those healing processes.

I learned to identify my patterns and my defense mechanisms. Along with my classwork I studied the specific work of child development experts like Penelope Leach and T. Berry Braselton to learn the specific developmental needs of boys. Once I learned those lessons, I used them to re-parent myself step by step, year by year, teaching myself the things I never learned from my mother or my father.

Along the way, I also learned something else: no one had taught me how to be a man—at least not a healthy man. I hadn't received a proper initiation into manhood from my father or from any of the other men in my life. If nobody showed me how to be a man, how was I supposed to know?

How is any boy supposed to know?

That question led to the Vision Quest I wrote about earlier. No experience in my life has been so powerful. I learned who I was. I learned about myself. I shared my deepest secrets and my pain, and I emerged healing and on the path to wholeness.

It took a group of men to teach me what it meant to be a man. This stayed with me. It gave me a vision of what I wanted to do with my future. I knew I had a mission in life to help other men heal their own wounds as I had. And I knew that I wanted to begin the healing when someone should have started the process with me—at the point of adolescence.

Healthy boys grow into healthy men. That's why I do what I do.

Index

A

absent fathers
  defined, 9
  effects of, 67, 133, 159
  emotionally absent fathers, 12–13
  example, 177
  "fun" dads, 11–12, 98
  Sam's example, 148
  statistics on, 10–11
absent parents, 134–136
abuse
  and the need for professional
    counseling, 60–61
  physical, 3–4, 110, 136–138, 160,
    177
  verbal, 75
acting out, 59, 75, 129
ADD/ADHD
  and anger, 77
  compared to PTSD, 16–18, 109,
    119
  medication for, 18–21, 111–112,
    125–126, 149
adolescence, as time of transition,
  145–146
adolescents, feelings experienced by,
  28–29
Andrew
  in counseling, 87
  future plans, 94–95
  medication, 87
  Obsessive Compulsive Disorder
    (OCD), 88, 90
  target of bullies, 85–87, 92, 94
  on The Quest Project®, 90–91, 93,
    95
  words of wisdom, 96
anger
  David's, 123
  dealing with, 61–63
  Dylan's, 74–76, 81
  Ethan's, 109–112
  expressing, 49–50, 61–63, 82, 84,
    116–117
  and sadness, 63–64, 76
  Sam's, 148–149
anger shadow, 61–62
anger song, 81, 116–117
anger work, 63–64
Asperger's Syndrome, 133
authorities, when to contact, 39, 157
author's experiences, 3–4, 177–180

B

bad influences, 24
behaviors, encouraging and
  discouraging, 40–41
boundaries, 81, 82, 83
Boy Scouts, influencing boys, 23–24
boys
  danger signals for, 2–3, 24, 97, 99,
    106
  encouraging, 37
  identifying their strengths, 66
  influences on, 14–15, 22, 23–24
Braselton, T. Berry, 179–180

bullying
    effects of, 85–89, 96, 162–163
    solutions for, 92

C

churches, influencing boys, 23
clean up, 60–61
coming-of-age rituals, 23
    See also initiation rituals
community support, 34–36
conflict resolution, 64–65, 82
container building, 55–57
counseling
    and Andrew, 87
    for boys, 60–61
    and David, 126–127
    and Dylan, 77
    and Ethan, 109–113
    and Joey, 164–165
    and Jordan, 103–104
    for parents, 43, 52–53, 56–57, 174
    for PTSD, 60–61
    and Sam, 150–151

D

Dad/Not Dad exercise, 65, 142
David
    anger, 125, 129
    in counseling, 126–127
    critical father, 124–125
    depression, 128
    drug use, 121–122, 125
    future plans, 130–131
    medication, 125, 126–127, 128
    parents' divorce, 122–123
    on the Quest Project®, 128–131
depression, 76, 128, 145, 146, 150,
    155–157, 179

divorce
    effects on David, 122–123
    effects on Dylan, 74–76
    effects on Sam, 150
    Kids in the Middle support
        group, 123
domestic violence, 3–4, 40, 110,
    136–137, 160, 177
"don't be" messages, 37, 62, 68, 128,
    162
drug use, 33–34, 50, 77, 122–123,
    125, 126, 178–179
Dylan
    anger, 74–75, 81, 82, 84
    background, 73–74
    in counseling, 77
    depression, 76–77
    and divorce, 74–76
    medication, 77, 83
    on The Quest Project®, 78–80, 83
    verbally abusive, 75

E

emotionally absent fathers. *See*
    absent fathers
Ethan, 109–119
    abuse, 109–110
    anger, 109–112, 116–117
    in counseling, 109, 113
    future plans, 119
    medication, 111–112, 118
    PTSD, 109, 113, 115, 119
    on the Quest Project®, 114–116,
        118
examples
    Andrew, 85–96
    David, 121–131
    Dylan, 73–84

Ethan, 109–119
first Quest Project® successes,
49–50, 51–52
Joey, 159–172
Jordan, 97–107
Sam, 147–157
Steven, 133–144
exercises
anger shadow, 61–62
anger work, 63–64
clean up, 60–61
conflict resolution, 64–65
container building, 56–57
Dad/Not Dad, 65
the Gift, 66
goal setting, 58
graduation from the Quest
Project®, 68–70
for parents, 5–7
purpose = mission, 68
relationships and forgiveness, 67
tool box, 58–60
visualization, 58, 60–61, 65–66,
153, 166–167
See also What Mom Can Do

F

fantasy parent exercise, 57
fantasy son exercise, 5–7, 173
fathers
being critical, 124–125, 159–160,
161
as mentors, 32, 35
statistics about, 10–11
See also absent fathers
fears, of parents, 77, 97–99, 121

feelings
discussing, 53
normalness of, 29, 32–34
forgiveness, 67
"fun" dads. *See* absent fathers;
perpetual adolescents

G

Gift exercise, 66
goal setting, 57–58, 70
graduation from the Quest Project®,
68–70
grandparents, advice for, 142–143
growing pains, 32–33
growing up
defined, 30–31
and pain, 29, 32–34, 58
guided imagery, 57

I

in-patient programs, 42–43
industrialization, and lack of male
role models, 30
initiation rituals, 35–37, 68–69
anger work, 63–64
Iron Hans, 66

J

Joey
abuse, 160–161
in counseling, 164–165
critical father, 159–162
depression, 163
future plans, 169–172
on the Quest Project®, 164–166
target of bullies, 161–162

Jordan
  absent father, 98
  in counseling, 103–104
  drug use, 99–102
  relationship with his mother,
    105–107
  on The Quest Project, ®, 104–105
journaling, for parents, 52

K

Kids in the Middle, 123

L

Leach, Penelope, 179–180

M

male role models
  examples, 98
  need for, 28, 173
manhood, transition to, 27, 31–37
medication
  for ADD/ADHD, 16, 18–21, 149
  prescribed for behavior problems,
    111–112, 125–126, 138
mentors, 31–32, 53
  and Dad/Not Dad exercise, 65
  need for, 131, 173
  See also role models
mission statements, 68
mothers
  boys separating from, 27–28
  See also parents; single mothers

N

natural consequences, 40–41, 53

O

Obsessive Compulsive Disorder
  (OCD), 88, 90

P

pain
  confronting, 48, 81, 115, 116–117,
    141, 171
  David's, 122–123, 125, 129
  dealing with, 58–60, 141, 167, 179
  and "don't be" messages, 128
  Ethan's, 112–113, 115–116
  of growing up, 29, 32–34
  Joey's, 166–167, 170
  for parents, 39–40, 51
  Sam's, 148–149
  Steven's, 134–135
parents
  aggressive behavior towards,
    39–40
  exercises to do, 5–7, 56–57
  fears of, 77, 97–99, 121
  feelings of failure, 39
  letting go, 105
  support groups for, 53
  working outside the home, 13
  See also What Mom Can Do
perpetual adolescents, 11–12, 29–30,
  98
  See also absent fathers
police, contacting, 39, 41
Pride Program, 46–47
processing feelings, 80

PTSD (Post Traumatic Stress
    Disorder)
    compared to ADD/ADHD,
        16–18, 119
    Ethan's example, 109, 113, 115,
        119
    need for professional counseling,
        60–61
punching bags, 50, 53, 59, 62, 63–64,
    81, 93
purpose = mission, 68

Q

quest project. *See* The Quest Project®

R

relationship officers, 41
relationships, 67
religion, as an influence on boys, 23

S

Sam, 147–157
    absent father, 148
    in counseling, 150–151
    depression, 146
    and divorce, 150
    and emotional control, 147
    medication, 149
    stealing, 148–149
    suicide risk, 146, 150–151
    on The Quest Project®, 152–154
schools, failing boys, 15–16
secret-keeping, 101–102
self-medicating, 33–34, 50, 77,
    122–123, 125–126, 178–179
single mothers, 9–10
    See also parents
sports, supporting boys, 22

stability, need for, 133–134, 136
statistics
    boys and school, 15–16
    on fathers, 10–11
    on suicide, 145–146
    stealing, 148–149
Steven, 133–144
    absent parents, 133–137
    anger, 135, 137
    medication, 133, 138
    on The Quest Project®, 140–142
    violent outbursts, 137–138, 139
suicide
    dealing with threats of, 39, 42–43,
        157
    and Sam, 150–151
    statistics on, 145–146
support from the other boys, 79,
    104–105, 114–115, 140, 166
support groups
    Kids in the Middle, 123
    for parents, 53

T

the big four, 53
The Quest Project®
    Andrew on, 90–91, 93, 95
    anger shadow, 61–63
    anger work, 63–64
    clean up, 60–61
    confidentiality, 80
    conflict resolution, 64–65
    container building, 55–57
    David on, 128–131
    Dylan on, 78–80, 83
    Ethan on, 114–116, 118
    evolution, 50–51
    expanding, 70

the Gift, 66
goal setting, 57–58
graduation, 68–70
Joey on, 164–166
Jordan on, 104–105
origins, 46–48
parent meetings, 50–51, 55, 59
purpose = mission, 68
relationships and forgiveness, 67
Sam on, 152–154
Steven on, 140–142
tool box, 58–60
theft, 148–149
threatening behavior, 39–42
   See also natural consequences
tool box, 58–60

U

understanding, and conflict
   resolution, 64–65

V

vision quests, 45–46, 57, 69, 180
visualization exercises, 58, 60–61,
   65–66, 153, 166–167

W

What Mom Can Do
   anger shadow, 62
   anger work, 64
   clean up, 60–61
   conflict resolution, 65
   container building, 56–57
   the Gift, 66
   goal setting, 58
   graduation from the Quest
      Project®, 68–70
   purpose = mission, 68
   relationships and forgiveness, 67
   tool box exercise, 59–60
   worksheets, conflict resolution, 65